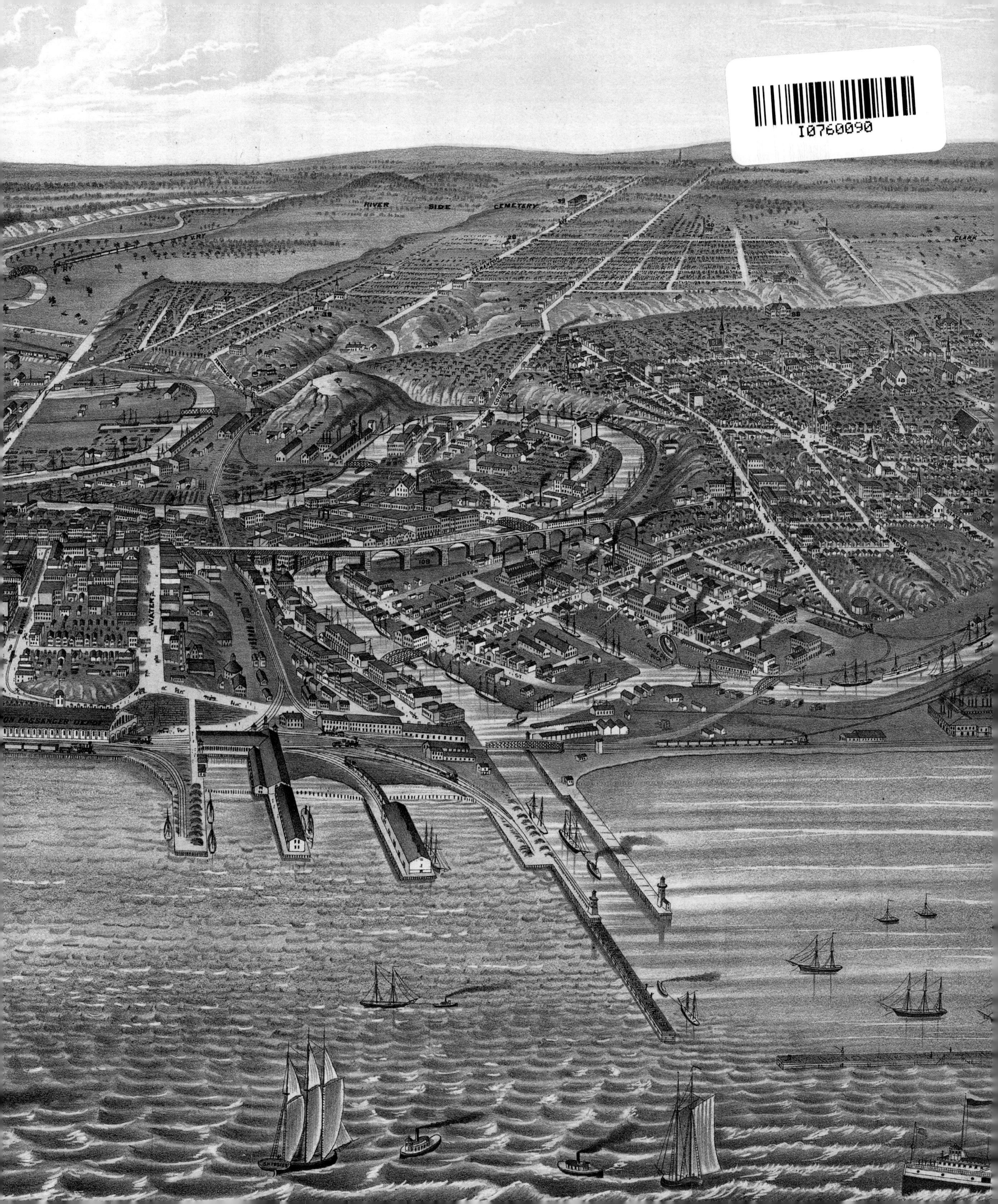
RIVER
SIDE
CEMETERY
WASHINGTON
CENTER
WATER
CLARK

Institute of Classical Architecture & Art
20 West 44th Street, Suite 310, New York, NY 10036
Telephone: (212) 730-9646 Facsimile: (212) 730-9649
www.classicist.org

Guest Editor: Jeffrey Tilman

Managing Editor: Stephanie Salomon
Design: Suzanne Ketchoyian

ISBN: 978-1-7330309-6-0
ISSN: 1077-2922

ACKNOWLEDGMENTS

The ICAA, the *Classicist* Committee, and the Guest Editor would like to thank the many individuals who have provided generous assistance with this issue. We are deeply grateful to our expert authors and photographers as well as to our anonymous peer reviewers. We owe a special debt of gratitude to David Ellison, who heads the ICAA's Ohio & Lake Erie Chapter, for his valuable contributions to this year's Notable Precedents and the bibliography in addition to his ongoing input and advice. We would also like to thank Julie Carpenter of the Cincinnati Chapter of the AIA for her assistance. Finally, we extend our gratitude to the members of the ICAA staff, who were essential to producing *Classicist* No. 22, in particular Julie Benton at the national office.

PHOTO CREDITS

Front cover: Cleveland Museum of Art, by Hubbell & Benes, 1916. View of southern facade, overlooking Wade Lagoon. Photo: Igor Oliyarnik

Back cover: Aerial view of Over-the-Rhine, Cincinnati. Photo: Ben Wright Photography

Front endpaper: Bird's-eye view of Cleveland, Ohio, 1877, by Albert Ruger; published by J. J Stoner and Shober & Carqueville, Madison, Wisconsin. Library of Congress

Back endpaper: Panoramic view of Cincinnati, Ohio, 1900, by John L. Trout and Henderson Lithographing Co., Cincinnati, Ohio. Library of Congress

Page 75: Detail of sculpture *Commerce* by Daniel Chester French at the Federal Building and U. S. Post Office (now the Howard M. Metzenbaum U. S. Courthouse), Cleveland, by Arnold Brunner, 1910. Terminal Tower (Graham, Anderson Probst & White, 1927) is in the background.

Page 91: Sculpture *Integrity* by Henry Hering, 1923, at the entrance to the Federal Reserve Bank of Cleveland by Walker & Weeks, 1921–23. Photo: Tim Evanson

Page 111: One of the eight sculptures *Guardians of Traffic*, Hope Memorial Bridge, Cleveland, by Henry Hering, 1932. Photo: Danita Delimont/Alamy Stock Photo

Printing: Allied Printing Services, Manchester, CT

CLASSICIST № 22

OHIO

LETTER FROM THE EDITOR

Why, Oh Why, Oh Why-O,
Why did I ever leave Ohio?
—Betty Comden and Adolph Green,
from *Wonderful Town*

In musical theater, Ohio is a place where Easterners believe they will be forsaken, lost in a sea of coal or corn. From *Wonderful Town* to *The Last Five Years*, Ohio is depicted as a place devoid of the opportunity and sophistication of the Eastern metropolises just over the Appalachians.

This characterization is relatively new, dating from the mid-twentieth century. Before then, Ohio was thought of as a place of unbounded prospects. The industrial economy of the United States would not have expanded as it did without the enterprise of Ohioans such as Thomas Edison, John D. Rockefeller, and the Wright Brothers. Ohio was an essential political power due to the election of seven Ohio presidents. And for many traveling north on the Underground Railroad, Ohio meant freedom—at least until the Dred Scott decision. Between the Civil War and the Roaring Twenties, Ohio was arguably the indispensable state.

With this prosperity, a building culture developed that valued order, permanence, and a continuity with the past. Ohio's early buildings were rooted in the classical tradition, marking the territory as a newly acquired outpost of the Western cultural sphere. William Heyer explores the meaning and craft of these early buildings in his essay on the state's exemplary Greek Revival architecture. Barbara Powers examines the evolution of the Ohio county courthouse as the type became a lasting symbol of small-town civic order. Robert Loversidge spent years studying and restoring the magnificent Ohio Statehouse, and in his essay, he shares his insights into the building's continuing resonance with the people of Ohio.

View of Over-the-Rhine, Cincinnati, from Mount Adams. Notable buildings include (from left to right) St. Paul's Church, Music Hall, Old St. Mary's Church, and Union Terminal (now the Cincinnati Museum Center).

One legacy of all those now-dead Ohio presidents is the several memorials built in their honor. Kay Fanning examines the meaning and sentiment behind these overscaled and sometimes overwrought classical memorials. Stephanie Ryberg-Webster and Thomas W. Hilde provide context for these monuments and much of Cleveland's civic building in their discussion of that city's Group Plan and the emergence of the University Circle cultural center. The development of the nearby community of Shaker Heights drove much of the growth along the Euclid Avenue corridor. Anne Steinert considers several of Ohio's most significant suburban developments and uncovers the means and the motivations behind those who settled there.

Many of Ohio's architects today work with the state's incredibly rich and voluminous building stock, specializing in rehabilitation and adaptive reuse. Given the state's tradition of excellence in the classical building arts, and as reflected in this issue's Professional Portfolio, it is not surprising that many of these architects have extended the classical language to meet today's needs. The Academic Portfolio offers inspiring evidence that the tradition will be taken up by the next generation of designers.

We are proud to be able to share some of Ohio's extraordinary architectural heritage in these pages, and I encourage you to visit the state. You'll find the rusty steel mills and the over-the-top tailgating you're expecting, but also vibrant, forward-looking cities, charming small towns, and a surprising variety of natural landscapes. You'll see architecture of the highest quality, as Ohioans have always lavished their considerable wealth on their homes, places of worship, and institutional buildings. For a moment, you might even consider staying. But when you do return to your own "Wonderful Town," don't be surprised if sometime later you catch yourself asking, "Why did I ever leave Ohio?"

Jeffrey Tilman
Guest Editor

Photo: © J. Miles Wolf

OHIO

THE ESSENTIAL STATE OF THE NINETEENTH CENTURY

JEFFREY TILMAN

Since World War II, Ohio has been more a place to be from than a place to be going to. The state became famous for all the people that had left, and then infamous to some as a place only worth flying over. Those who never set foot in the state are missing out on seeing one of the nation's richest and most varied collections of architecture and landscapes, much of it the product of a time when Ohio was the economic engine and political bellwether of the entire nation. What California was to the United States in the twentieth century, Ohio was in the nineteenth century. From statehood in 1803 through the Roaring 1920s, Ohio was at the center of the nation's economic, political, and cultural life, and its citizens built communities, large, middling, and small, that reflected the prosperity of the age and a confidence in the American democratic project.

OHIO BEFORE STATEHOOD

The earliest Ohioans, the Native peoples, began Ohio's building history. The people now known as the Adena and the Hopewell constructed complex earthworks aligned with the phases of the eighteen-year lunar cycle, such as those at Newark, Ohio; these are now designated as World Heritage sites. The well-known effigy mound the Great Serpent, in Adams County, likely dates from c. 1050 CE, which suggests that the Fort Ancient peoples built it. These civilizations, temporally separate from each other, had disappeared by CE 1200, making space for the modern tribes associated with the state—the Miami, the Wyandot, and the Shawnee. When the Continental Army won the Revolutionary War, the United Kingdom ceded its lands south of the Great Lakes to the new United States, which immediately opened these lands to white settlement. The Shawnee and Miami resisted this incursion into their lands, but with their defeat at the Battle of Fallen Timbers in 1794 and their accession to the Treaty of Greenville the following year, they were forced to resettle to the west. By 1840, the federal and state governments recognized no tribal lands anywhere in the state, a situation that remains to this day.

Fig 1. LeVeque Tower, Columbus, by C. Howard Crane, 1923.

The lands the Native peoples left behind were quickly claimed by speculators from the eastern states. The Land Ordinance of 1785 called for the Ohio Country to be divided into townships, sections, and finally 640-acre lots. One-seventh of these lands were reserved as compensation for Revolutionary War veterans who were still owed their service and enlistment bounties. Four sections of each township were reserved by the federal government for future speculative sale, and one section's income was to be used to support a public school. The lands to the north were similarly mapped for quick sale. For years, Connecticut had pressed its claims to the lands along Lake Erie west of Pennsylvania, called the Western Reserve. In 1786, Connecticut settled its claim on the territory, ceding control to the federal government but retaining ownership of the lands, which the state then sold to the Connecticut Land Company. A somewhat similar process occurred to the south, in the lands bordering the Ohio River, where Manasseh Cutler and Rufus Putnam of Massachusetts organized the Ohio Land Company. In 1787, the group purchased 900,000 acres along the Ohio River, and in the following year Putnam constructed a wood fort, somewhat romantically called the Campus Martius, and then established the town of Marietta, the first American community to be founded in Ohio. Now part of the Campus Martius Museum, Putnam's house remains the oldest extant building in the state. The house was located next to the fort and constructed in the post-and-plank manner common to Federal-era houses in New England. Work on the house begun immediately after Putnam arrived and was largely complete by 1790.[1]

Photo: Ohio History Connection

Fig. 2. Adena, Thomas Worthington Estate, Chillicothe, by Benjamin Henry Latrobe, 1807.

The primary settlers from the South were Virginians. Settlers poured into the region through the Cumberland Gap into Kentucky and then northward across the Ohio River. The land between the Great and Little Miami Rivers was known as Symmes Purchase, named for Judge John Cleves Symmes. In 1787, his consortium acquired 300,000 acres and constructed communities along the Ohio River between the Miami Rivers; among these was Losantiville, which was renamed the following year by Northwest Territory Governor Arthur St. Clair as Cincinnati, in honor of the Society of the Cincinnati.

STATEHOOD AND THE CANAL ERA: 1800–1840

The communities along the Ohio River and up the Greater Miami and Scioto Rivers were the first to draw significant population, and the years between the founding of Marietta and Cincinnati and 1800 saw both communities grow into respectable port towns. But growth really took off in Ohio with statehood. In 1800, the non-Native population of the entire Northwest Territories was 46,000; by 1810, the population of Ohio alone was 230,000.[2] This explosive growth would continue throughout the nineteenth century and into the twentieth, ensuring that Ohio would remain a critical player in the nation's development.

Ohio statehood was authorized by the Enabling Act of 1802.[3] The new state's constitution was presented to Congress by Thomas Worthington the following January, and Congress accepted Ohio into the Union on February 19, 1803. Worthington became the state's first U.S. senator that September. The architectural community remembers Worthington largely for his manor house, designed by Benjamin Henry Latrobe in 1805, and now called "Adena," from which the ancient Native peoples were named. Worthington had worked with Latrobe on the completion of the U.S. Capitol. Thus, when Worthington decided to replace the log home he had built at Chillicothe, he naturally chose Latrobe to be the architect.[4]

Adena is in some ways typical of Latrobe's program for the American house, and in other ways it deviates from much of the architect's work. The building is quite blocky, built of sandstone with little to no exterior ornamentation (fig. 2). The essential form is Palladian, as the road elevation is dominated by two hipped-roofed rectangular service wings placed astride the two story, five-bay main block, joined not by hyphens, but by the barest overlap of the two. A colonnaded porch raised on a plinth runs between the two wings. The columns are spindly and barely hint at the Greco-Roman orders. The garden facade was intended to be the showpiece of the place. Here the facade is only three bays wide and very similar to others by Latrobe, such as at the Pope Villa in Lexington, Kentucky. The interior of Adena does not have the elaborate multistory architectural promenade of Latrobe's Decatur House, and the trim and casework of the principal rooms are spare and clearly executed by local craftsmen.

Worthington was Ohio's most important politician throughout the state's first twenty years, becoming governor after serving as senator.[5] He set the course for the state's future development early on, when he

Photo: Philip Groshong, courtesy of the Taft Museum of Art

Fig. 3. Baum-Taft House, now Taft Museum of Art, Cincinnati, built 1820.

proposed a feasibility study for a nationwide canal system that would link the Hudson River to Lake Erie and the lake to the Ohio River, and thus to the Mississippi and the Louisiana Territory. DeWitt Clinton was put in charge of the project, and he saw the Erie Canal through to completion. Worthington committed Ohio to being New York's partner in the venture; surveying for the Ohio and Erie Canal began in 1822, and construction began three years later. By 1833, the entire 300-mile-long canal system was operational. A parallel project, the Miami-Erie Canal, linked Cincinnati to Dayton along the Great Miami River. This system was extended northward in the 1840s through Troy and Defiance to the Maumee River and on to the lake at Toledo.

Although the canal system was quickly supplanted by the railroads, the two canals made nearly every corner of Ohio an inland port. The state's unusually even population distribution is largely a result of the canals built two centuries ago. Towns built along the canals thrived as entrepots for more inland locales, and the termini, particularly at Cleveland, Toledo, and Cincinnati, developed into major manufacturing centers. The state and its investors may have been dismayed at the canal system's seemingly sudden obsolescence, but the emerging rail industry repurposed much of the canal rights-of-way. In the mid-twentieth century, these same rights-of-way were used in part to build parts of the interstate highways that link the urban centers together today.

EARLY CINCINNATI

Cincinnati perhaps benefited from the construction of the canals more than any other city. It became a primary center for commercial traffic along the Ohio River as well as from the Miami Valley. Within a decade of its founding, the hamlet had become a town of 2,500 people. This population more than doubled with each decade until the 1840s, when the failed revolutions in central Europe sent a wave of German-speaking immigrants into the city, to the point where in 1850 Cincinnati was the sixth-largest city in the United States, with a population of nearly 120,000.[6]

The first buildings in Cincinnati were simple wooden structures, but these gave way within twenty years to brick warehouses and commercial buildings along the waterfront. None of these early commercial buildings survive. The city's oldest structure, the William Betts House, was built of local brick in 1804, and originally was three bays wide, with only one room on each of its two floors. This building is very similar to town houses constructed in Betts's native New Jersey, and by the 1820s a tradition of detached brick town houses made up most of Cincinnati's housing stock.

The exceptional houses were on larger lots at the edges of the city grid. The Martin Baum House, today's Taft Museum of Art, was constructed as a one-story Federal-style pavilion similar in form to Homewood in Baltimore or Bremo in Virginia (fig. 3). These pavilion houses were found in some number in Kentucky, and a few were built across the river in Ohio, including Spread Eagle Tavern in Butler County, northeast of Cincinnati. Baum came to Cincinnati around 1789, ran a series of successful businesses, was once elected mayor, and in 1820 built his dream house on Pike Street, just at the edge of the town's limits. The five-bay, hipped-roofed main block of the house is flanked by four-bay wings on each side. The entry is sheltered by a central portico supported by coupled Tuscan columns. The second story of the center block is suppressed under the hip roof, appearing to be a mezzanine lit by elliptical windows. Baum lost his fortune in an economic depression that began in 1826, and he had to sell his trophy home to pay off his debts. The interior of the building underwent a great number of changes as a result, the most significant of which was to transform the home into an art museum.[7]

Photo: Nagel Photography/Shutterstock

Fig. 4. Isaac M. Wise Temple, Cincinnati, by James Keyes Wilson, 1863.

CINCINNATI'S BOOM YEARS OF RIVER AND RAIL: 1840–1865

The growth of Cincinnati in the 1840s and '50s led to the development of the city's distinctive residential type, and this growth drew to the city a number of nationally prominent architects. As the city moved north of the Miami-Erie Canal, the building stock transitioned from Federal and Greek Revival buildings to Italianate iron-front commercial buildings and tenements. Throughout the middle decades of the nineteenth century, Cincinnati supported a number of iron foundries that specialized in architectural elements. Thus, most of the iron-front buildings in the city's Over-the-Rhine neighborhood are truly homegrown, composed of locally sourced brick and timber, and faced with locally manufactured facades. Perhaps the best of these commercial buildings was constructed for the German Mutual Insurance Company, designed by local architect Johann Bast in 1877 (fig. 5). This four-story building's Dayton limestone facade is dominated by an allegorical statue of "Germania" by Leopold Gettweis. Above this, an enormous bracketed arched sheet-metal cornice, manufactured by L. Schreiber and Sons, defines the skyline. The most celebrated building in Cincinnati in the latter half of the nineteenth century must have been the now-demolished Burnet Hotel, designed by Isaiah Rogers in 1848. Rogers designed a six-story building containing over 340 rooms; the building was crowned with a forty-two-foot-diameter dome that rose 140 feet above the street. Upon completion it was deemed by some to be "the finest hotel in the world."[8]

Several of the best surviving examples of classicism in Cincinnati are Roman Catholic churches. The oldest extant church in the city is Old St. Mary's, a congregation initiated in 1840 specifically to address the needs of Over-the-Rhine's German-speaking population. Designed by Franz Erd, the church was completed by 1842 and is distinctive for its multi-stage bell tower that soars more than 150 feet over the building's Greek Revival facade. At the same time the Roman Catholic community was also building city's most impressive Greek Revival church, the Cathedral Basilica of St. Peter in Chains, today the oldest purpose-built cathedral church in the United States (see p. 28). Designed by Henry Walter in 1841–42 and clearly inspired by James Gibbs's St. Martin-in-the-Fields, the church sits on a story-high stepped podium at the corner of Eighth and Plum Streets.[9]

Cincinnati's most significant Jewish house of worship is the Isaac M. Wise Temple, directly across Plum Street from St. Peter in Chains (fig. 4). Wise, the most prominent Reform rabbi in the United States, wanted a building that would be the equal of its neighbor. His architect, James Keyes Wilson, overlaid Moorish and Islamic elements onto a fundamentally Gothic Revival plan. The materiality and strong use of color remind one of the contemporary English Gothic Revival of the Oxford Movement, while the twin octagonal towers rising out of the roof are clearly Wilson's own invention.

Photo: Brian Zehowski

Fig. 5. German Mutual Insurance Company Building, Over-the-Rhine, Cincinnati, by Johann Bast, 1877.

The Isaac M. Wise Temple is indicative of a great deal of Cincinnati institutional architecture between the 1850s and 1900. Although most commercial structures were some form of Italianate, and thus had some link to the classical tradition, the majority of public buildings—Samuel Hannaford's City Hall and Music Hall, H. H. Richardson's Chamber of Commerce Building, James McLaughlin's reworking of Walter and Wilson's Hamilton County Courthouse, and nearly all of the schools—were designed in the Romanesque or Gothic Revival styles. Of course, these forms were popular across the United States for most of the post–Civil War period. But one might speculate that because of Cincinnati's very large German population, the styles that were prevalent in Central Europe, popularized in the German architectural press by Heinrich Hübsch and Gottfried Semper, found particular favor in Cincinnati. Hannaford, the city's most prominent architect of the postwar period, was certainly comfortable in medieval styles, and, being originally from England, knew many of the sources of the American Gothic Revival firsthand.

ARCHITECTURAL INNOVATION IN CINCINNATI: 1865–1935

The years between the Civil War and the Great Depression saw massive change in the American landscape and in daily life. Cincinnati was very often at the forefront of innovation in design, particularly with regard to incorporating new materials into traditional building.

The most famous of these innovative projects was the Cincinnati-Covington Bridge, John A. Roebling's suspension bridge over the Ohio River. At over 1,000 feet long, it was the longest single-span bridge in the world at its completion in 1867. Another important landmark in structural engineering came ten years later with the completion of Shillito's Department Store on Seventh and Race Streets. James McLaughlin's design for the awkward L-shaped site set an octagonal atrium the entire height of the building just inside the angle of the L. This way, a huge skylight could light much of the individual floors and allow the public to see what was on each of them (fig. 8). Such a building required an iron frame, yet iron had proven calamitous during the Great Chicago Fire of 1871. McLaughlin brought into the office William Le Baron Jenney. He wrapped each iron column with a brick jacket; the only place where the iron was exposed was at the atrium, where the columns were completely independent of the rest of the structure and supported only the skylight. Jenney returned to Chicago in 1879 and reused this system, and the exterior elevation he designed with McLaughlin, in the First Leiter Building, the forerunner of the Chicago Frame building and of many department stores worldwide.[10]

Photo: Ian Dagnall/Alamy Stock Photo

Fig. 6. Ingalls Building, Cincinnati, by Elzner & Anderson; Henry N. Hooper, structural engineer, 1903.

Innovation in Cincinnati also extended to concrete construction. The Ingalls Building (now Courtyard by Marriott), designed by local firm Elzner & Anderson, was the world's tallest concrete-framed building at its construction (fig. 6). Its developer, Melville E. Ingalls, and his structural engineer and contractor, Henry N. Hooper, believed that Ernest Ransome's system of barbed reinforcing bars would fuse the floor, column, and wall elements into one single structural unit, resisting both the gravity loads and the wind loads borne by the building. After a successful two-year campaign to gain a building permit for the sixteen-story tower, the building rose quickly over the latter half of 1903. The exterior was clad in marble and terra cotta to give the building a refined Classical Revival finish, and the interiors were complete enough for the building to open in March 1904.[11]

The Ingalls Building would be dwarfed by its eventual neighbor, Carew Tower, and the adjoining Netherland Plaza Hotel. The mixed-use complex at Fifth and Vine Streets was the brainchild of John Emory, whose mother, Marie, had financed Mariemont, John Nolen's planned community just east of Cincinnati. Emory's vision for a "city within a city" was not shared by his bankers. In the end, he was forced to self-finance much of the project and so liquidated his entire stock portfolio in September 1929 to support the project. Of course, within weeks his action proved fortuitous, and with the deflation of the Great Depression, Carew Tower came in at a cost of thirty million dollars.

The project was programmed and constructed by Emory's partner, William A. Starrett, whose firm was also constructing the Empire State Building. It eventually contained the 49-story main tower, a 600-room hotel, and a 27-story parking tower that was served by elevators (fig. 7). All were designed by Walter W. Ahlschlager of Chicago in association with the New York firm of Delano & Aldrich, who had designed Emory's home "Peterloon" in nearby Indian Hill. The steel frame went up at the astonishing rate of a story a day, setting a record. The rest of the construction went at an equally breakneck speed; the entire project was completed in just thirteen months. Today the tower, its shopping arcade, and especially the hotel, are noted for their Art Deco interiors. Although the hotel was "modernized" in the 1960s, later restoration efforts were able to reveal the amazing murals by Louis Grell and sculptures by Rene Paul Chambellan in the Fountain Court, as well as the Rookwood detail in the ceilings in the Hall of Mirrors.

Fig. 7. Carew Tower and Netherland Plaza Hotel, Cincinnati, by Walter W. Ahlschlager and Delano & Aldrich, 1929–30.

Perhaps the city's most well-known building is Union Terminal, now the Museum Center of Cincinnati (fig. 9). After numerous floods in the early twentieth century, the city's railroads agreed to develop a unified rail terminal in Cincinnati. In 1927, they hired New York architects Alfred T. Fellheimer and Steward Wagner to design a logical and efficient layout for the complex circulation of the facility, but their design of the building seemed dated. The directors demanded that their rail terminal be as forward-looking as possible, and they hired Paul Philippe Cret to rework the architectural character of the project.[12] What this team of architects came up with is one of the most significant Art Deco buildings on Earth. From the 110-foot-high concrete half dome down to the silverware used in the café, every element of the building was harmoniously steeped in the new "modernistic" design language. As it did at the terminal's opening in 1933, the Rotunda remains the breathtaking center of the building. The Winold Reiss murals, greater than life-size, of the city's development and the evolution showing transportation, line the back of the entire room. Now the Museum Center for all of Hamilton County, Union Terminal embodies the spirit of Cincinnati at

Photo: Courtesy of Jeffrey Tilman

Fig. 8. Interior atrium of Shillito's Department Store (now Lofts at Shillito Place), Cincinnati, by James McLaughlin and William Le Baron Jenney, 1877.

the city's most successful and optimistic. Its decline and rebirth into a treasured landmark mirror the challenges the city experienced in the second half of the twentieth century.

CLEVELAND'S RISE TO NATIONAL PROMINENCE: THE CIVIL WAR AND LATE NINETEENTH CENTURY

The Civil War had a profound effect on Ohio, just as it did everywhere else in the nation. Ohioans served in enormous numbers for the Union cause; it is thought that 60 percent of the able-bodied men of fighting age served in uniform during the conflict. The state delivered the third-largest contingent of men to the Grand Army of the Republic, and the most notable and successful generals of that army, Ulysses S. Grant, William Tecumseh Sherman, and Philip H. Sheridan, were Ohioans.

The state was rewarded for this service with enormous political power. In the sixty years from the end of the war in 1865, fully seven Ohioans were elected to the presidency, serving for a total of twenty-eight years. (This would have been more if James Garfield, William McKinley, and Warren Harding hadn't died in office.) With its close ties to the Republican Party, and with its indispensable electoral votes, nearly 15 percent of those needed to win, it is not surprising that Ohio, and particularly northern Ohio, had an outsized role to play in national politics all through the second half of the nineteenth and early twentieth centuries.

The Civil War sparked Cleveland's transformation into an industrial powerhouse, but it would be several decades before the city's name would be nearly synonymous with heavy industry. While many companies supplied the Union Army with equipment and armaments during the war, this was not yet done at scale. The city's iron foundries were successful during the 1860s and 1870s, but far greater profits came once the foundries were converted to steel production, (the Cleveland Rolling Mill Company was making steel by 1868), and they were vertically integrated with other sites across the Midwest. For example, the iron ore was shipped from northern Minnesota to Cleveland through the Great Lakes system. Coal to power the blast furnaces came from western Pennsylvania and later West Virginia. Clays and other minerals came from the south-central counties of Ohio and were delivered north on railroads that followed the old Ohio-Erie Canal. Once all these resources were gathered under the umbrella of one company, all that was left to make unheard-of profits was to control the transportation of these materials and the finished product as they were brought to market.

Standard Oil of Ohio, formally organized in 1870, was more than happy to consolidate the transportation of nearly anything that moved by land or lake in Ohio, Pennsylvania, and the Mid-Atlantic states. Oil was the center of the John D. Rockefeller's commercial octopus, and Rockefeller made Cleveland the unquestioned center of American oil production and refining in the years before the turn of the twentieth century. The Standard Oil Trusts also controlled numerous shipping

Photo: Michael Fitzsimmons/Alamy Stock Photo

Fig. 9. Union Terminal, Cincinnati, by Alfred T. Fellheimer and Steward Wagner with design input from Paul Philippe Cret, 1927–33.

companies and railroads, initially to move oil, but later for their own sake. Rockefeller moved his family to New York City in 1884, so when the Ohio Supreme Court ruled that the Standard Oil Trusts should be broken up in 1892, Rockefeller moved nearly all his assets into shell companies out of state, largely into Standard Oil of New Jersey.[13] Today few Americans realize that the Rockefeller fortune was generated first out of Ohio.

But Cleveland wasn't just built on oil and steel—the city had a number of other industrial assets, including several major chemical companies. Eugene Ramiro Grasselli founded a branch of his Cincinnati-based chemical company in Cleveland to serve the Rockefeller oil refineries in 1867. Soon he was buying out his local competitors on his way to establishing a conglomerate of chemical plants that spread across six states. All through the 1890s, the city was home to dozens of automobile start-ups. By World War I, however, the city had lost its leadership in the automobile industry, as Henry Ford, the Dodge Brothers, and Ransom Olds consolidated the industry in Detroit. Cleveland remained important to the industry, but largely for the manufacture of parts and for some final assembly.

Cleveland was host to a number of early electrical equipment manufacturers, many of which were bought out by Edison's General Electric. Charles F. Brush was an early electrical engineer who developed a dynamo capable of generating a large amount of electrical energy. He created an outdoor lighting system using arc-lamps that was used to light Public Square in 1879. Around a decade later, he founded the Arcade Company of Cleveland, Ohio. With funding from Mark Hanna and

Photo: Jose Luis Stephens/Alamy Stock Photo

Fig. 10. Severance Hall, Cleveland, by Walker & Weeks, 1931.

John D. Rockefeller, the new company commissioned George H. Smith and John Eisenmann to design nineteenth-century Cleveland's most beloved building, the Cleveland Arcade (see p. 63).[15]

All this industrial growth attracted hundreds of thousands of people to Cleveland in the decades around the turn of the twentieth century. By 1900, Cleveland surpassed Cincinnati as the state's largest city; its population would peak at just over 900,000 inhabitants in 1950. Immigrants from Southern and Eastern Europe, particularly Germany, Hungary, Russia, and Italy, flocked to northern Ohio to take positions in the steel industry, and in related manufacturing. Black Americans moved north to many of Ohio's cities during the Great Migration for the better-paying jobs large-scale industry could provide.

CITY BEAUTIFUL CLEVELAND: 1900–30

Many of Cleveland's tycoons worked toward the betterment of the city's infrastructure and civic life. The most significant of these efforts is undoubtedly the implementation of the Group Plan of 1903 and the creation of the University Circle cultural district along Doan Brook to the east; these centers of redevelopment, joined by Euclid Avenue, became the focus of the City Beautiful Movement in Cleveland in the first three decades of the twentieth century.

Cleveland's redevelopment of its waterfront northeast of Public Square represents the most comprehensive realization of the City Beautiful Movement's ideals in Ohio. Inspired by the World's Columbian Exposition of 1893 in Chicago and the recent proposals illustrated in the Senate Park Commission Plan for Washington, DC (the McMillan Plan), Cleveland's most important industrialists and landholders hired Daniel Burnham, Arthur Brunner, and John M. Carrère to develop a plan for the improvement to the city's waterfront along Lake Erie, and to link that redevelopment to Public Square through a series of landscaped malls. Seven prominent public buildings were to share a common classical language, scale, cornice heights, and materials, in a reinterpretation of the "White City" of the World's Fair. Unlike many of these efforts across the country, Cleveland largely executed this dream Civic Center, and by 1931 these new facilities did indeed reach the lakeshore.

The University Circle cultural district emerged on the eve of World War I. In 1906, it was decided to locate the Cleveland Museum of Art in Doan Park, southeast of the city center. The first phase of the building was designed by Cleveland firm Hubbell & Benes and was completed in 1916. The building was impressive; clad in a gleaming Georgia marble, it sits on a high basement. The central portico is in the Greek Ionic order of the Erechtheion, the pediment is crowned with acroteria, and subtly projected end pavilions feature broad sculpture niches (see p. 65).[16] Just south of the museum, along Euclid Avenue, lies the Severance Music Center (or Hall), home of the Cleveland Symphony Orchestra since its construction in 1931. Designed by Walker & Weeks, Severance Hall sits on a trapezoidal site, and this determined the plan of the building, which spreads out like a fan from a semi-octagonal entry element to the auditorium and a recital hall. The classical exterior is clad in limestone in sympathy with the surrounding arts district, while the interior received a much more modernistic treatment that we now call Art Deco (fig. 10).

Euclid Avenue serves as the link between the Group Plan and the University Circle District and continues on to the planned suburb of Shaker Heights. This community was developed from 1905 on by brothers Oris Paxton and Mantis James Van Sweringen to be the first Garden City suburb in the United States, following the dictates of Ebenezer Howard. To bring a high-speed streetcar line from their development into downtown Cleveland, and to thus attract the well-to-do clientele they desired, the brothers found themselves owning or controlling five railroads, inadvertently becoming one of the largest operators of railroads in the nation.

The terminus of the brothers' streetcar line was a site just southwest of Public Square. The Van Sweringens

Photo: iStock.com/benedek

Fig. 11. Terminal City, Cleveland, by Graham, Probst, Anderson & White, 1927.

owned the key landholdings for a union station serving all of the city's railroads, and in 1923 ground was broken for Cleveland Union Terminal City, a multimodal, multiuse retail, office, and shopping complex dominated by Terminal Tower; all was designed by the Chicago firm of Graham, Probst, Anderson & White (fig. 11). Terminal Tower rises fifty-two floors above the street and is turned forty-five degrees to emphasize its relationship to the diagonal of Public Square. The building was well received by critics at its opening in 1928, and for a while it was the symbol of a Cleveland that was taking its place among the nation's great cities.

Unfortunately, by the time the railroad terminus was completed, the bottom had fallen out of the stock market. The Van Sweringen brothers, their railroad empire highly leveraged, had to sell their assets; by the depths of the Depression, they had nearly nothing left and both were dead by 1936. Their legacy, however, lies with the model suburb of Shaker Heights, and the Tower Terminal complex, still the symbolic star of Cleveland's skyline.

THE REWARDS OF INDUSTRY: CLASSICAL REVIVAL MONUMENTS IN OHIO'S MID-SIZED CITIES

Ohio's cities were primed for industrial expansion in the years after the Civil War. At its peak at the turn of the twentieth century, Ohio was the second-largest producer of steel, with the industry concentrated in Cleveland, Youngstown, Lorain, and farther south, in Middletown. These large complexes naturally spawned auxiliary industries, such as the chemical industry in Cleveland, the automobile parts industries that dominated Canton, or the North American rubber industry, which was completely concentrated in Akron. In all these cities, the industrialist class built exceptional residences, often in the Tudor Revival style. F. A. Seiberling's Stan Hywet Hall in Akron (fig. 13), designed in 1911 for the co-founder of the Goodyear Tire Company by Cleveland architect Charles Sumner Schneider, is a stellar example of the Country Place movement. The sprawling Tudor house is set in spectacular gardens designed by Boston architect Warren Manning.

Dayton's most famous sons, the Wright Brothers, did not follow the vogue for the medieval. Enjoying fame and success as co-founders of the aviation industry, the brothers hired the local architectural firm Schenck & Williams to design a nine-bay, buff brick Classical Revival home in the city's Oakwood neighborhood. The house, Hawthorn Hill, is very much a trophy home, with an imposing two-story tetrastyle portico in the Scamozzi Ionic and Roman Doric porches at each end (fig. 14). Unfortunately, Wilbur Wright died in 1912 as the building was being planned, and eventually Orville lived in the sprawling home alone until

Photo: © Dayton Ohio Photos, Kevin L Myers

Fig. 12. Dayton Arcade, constructed 1902.

Photo: niagara66, CC BY-SA 4.0

Fig. 13. Stan Hywet Hall, Akron, by F.A. Seiberling, 1911.

Photo: Stan Rohrer/Alamy Stock Photo

Fig. 14. Hawthorn Hill, Dayton, by Schenk & Williams, 1912–14.

his death in 1948. The house was then bought by the National Cash Register Corporation to serve as a guest house for visiting dignitaries and thus preserved for the next sixty years.[17]

A number of Dayton's public buildings are also very much worth noting. The Dayton Arcade was created as a multibuilding commercial venture in 1902. The Third Street arcade is a two-story skylit Renaissance Revival shopping street fronted by a four-story Flemish Renaissance Revival gatehouse. This leads to the Rotunda, a three-story arcaded market hall lit by an enormous glass dome (fig. 12). After years of abandonment, a joint venture with the University of Dayton and a group of developers based in Baltimore rehabilitated the complex, which now houses retail, hospitality, office, and residential uses.[18]

The Dayton Art Institute is certainly one of the city's architectural jewels, and one of the leading regional museums in the nation. The museum sits on a bluff overlooking the Great Miami River, with a set of broad stairs leading up to the Renaissance Revival building. Designed by Edward Brodhead Green of Buffalo, New York, in 1930 as an Italian villa with extended wings, the primary elevation presents a five-bay stone block into which is set an arcaded loggia that sat above the original entry (fig. 15). Green also designed the main building for the Toledo Museum of Art (fig. 16). Instead of Renaissance repose and solemnity, at Toledo, Green employed a majestic, if perhaps overwhelming, Greek Revival. Completed quite a bit earlier than Dayton's museum, in 1912, the building is reached at the Monroe Street front by stepped terraces, and both the east and west facades are embellished with a colonnade of sixteen Ionic columns set in muris to give the impression of an ancient stoa. In 1933, Green added wings to each end of the building that more than doubled the gallery space of the museum. The South Pavilion contains a Greek theater that seats 1,750 patrons among twenty-eight Ionic columns arranged in a peristyle.

COLUMBUS IN THE NINETEENTH CENTURY: A GROWING CAPITOL CITY

From the time of statehood, many in Ohio wanted the capitol to be located at a site near the geographic center of the state.[19] Several locations in Franklin County were suggested, and when in 1812 the citizens of Franklintown offered up two sections of land for a statehouse and a prison, Governor Worthington signed legislation effectuating the move, once temporary housing for the government could be constructed. This was done by 1816, when the state legislatures met in the newly created town of Columbus for the first time.

Columbus did not take off in population like Cleveland or Cincinnati. In fact, Columbus didn't exceed Cleveland in population until sometime in 1985, and only because the city annexed most of Franklin Country starting in the 1950s. Columbus was not directly connected to the canal system until the 1830s, and a cholera epidemic greatly damaged the town's development and reputation. The design and construction of the Ohio Statehouse was extremely contentious, lasting eighteen years, and until the building was completed, many believed the capital might be moved somewhere else. That notwithstanding, with the extension of the National Road to Columbus in 1833, and, more important, with the construction of the Wheeling Suspension Bridge in 1849, Columbus found itself at the crossroads between the Eastern Seaboard and the ever-developing Midwest.

The towns located along the National Road naturally found themselves teeming with settlers from farther east, particularly from Pennsylvania and New Jersey. These settlers were primarily farmers, not tradesmen or manufacturers such as those who settled along the Ohio River or along Lake Erie. A distinctive farmhouse type emerged in these middle counties of Ohio that was codified by anthropologist Fred Kniffen as the "I-House."[20] This two-story house type was one room deep with two rooms on each floor separated by a central passage and stair. Rarely were these houses completed by professional builders before the Civil War, and details that denoted the orders might be purchased from several sources and installed without reference to the pattern books by Asher Benjamin or A. J. Downing that informed the work of the better class of rural building.

Despite this agricultural context, the primary purpose and raison d'être of the city of Columbus in the nineteenth century was to be the seat of state government (see the essay on the Ohio Statehouse in this volume, p. 43). Many of the best examples of the classical tradition in Columbus are associated with the builders of the

Photo: iStock.com/Stan Rohrer

Fig. 15. Dayton Art Institute, by Edward Brodhead Green, 1930.

Photo: Christopher Riley

Fig. 16. Toledo Museum of Art, by Edward Brodhead Green, 1912, expanded 1933.

Fig. 17. Benjamin E. Smith House, Columbus, by Nathan B. Kelley, 1866.

Statehouse and those in government. The Benjamin E. Smith House, next to the Capitol on East Broad Street (now the Columbus Club) was constructed in the years immediately after the Civil War (fig. 17). Smith, a railroad magnate who had profited handsomely from federal contracts during the war, asked Nathan B. Kelley, one of the architects of the Statehouse, to design his residence. Smith spared no expense; he went so far as to import the bricks from a brickyard in Philadelphia, each brick individually wrapped like a precious morsel of pastry. The resulting building was very grand for its time and place.

Before his dismissal from the Statehouse project, Kelley was one of Columbus's most important architects. His first important state commission was the Columbus State Hospital, an enormous four-story pile with a central portico and domed lobby at the entrance; this facility burned in 1868. Kelley also designed the first Franklin County Courthouse, and in 1862 he designed the first Central High School. Few of Kelley's numerous works survive today, and, in fact, visitors to Columbus may be left with the impression that the city emerged ex novo around 1890 or so. This is in part due to the devastating flood of the Scioto River in 1913, which wiped out most development along and west of the river, including all of Franklintown. Late-twentieth-century urban renewal efforts also erased a great deal of evidence of Columbus's past.

COLUMBUS AFTER THE 1913 FLOOD

The redevelopment of Columbus after the Great Flood of 1913 had to wait out World War I and the 1918 influenza epidemic. By 1920, civic boosters were ready to do something big. This came in the form of the American Insurance Union (AIU). The group bought a lot at Broad and Front Streets in Columbus in 1923 and hired Detroit architect C. Howard Crane to design a multibuilding retail, office, hotel, and entertainment complex (see fig. 1). The resulting forty-seven-story tower was complemented by eighteen-story wings. Topping off at 350,000 square feet of rentable space, the AIU Building was well beyond what the local economy could absorb. With the Great Depression, the American Insurance Union went into receivership. The tower sat largely empty until after World War II, when it was purchased by Leslie LeVeque and John Lincoln.

Although what is today known as the LeVeque Tower is often thought of as an Art Deco building, its design predates the introduction of that style, and Crane seems to have looked at late Roman and Byzantine models for the building, particularly for the crowning stories. That said, the tower is a unique creation. As it only occupies the southeast corner of the site, and since the corners are chamfered up to the stout circular buttresses near the crown, it appears wonderfully slender against the sky. The curved gables at the centers of the facades recall the form of a contemporary radio set, while on either side enormous figures stand guard at the corners. Above these one finds the observation deck at the forty-fourth floor and then the heavily ornamented dome.

The ground floor of the building contained retail spaces and the Keith Albee Theatre, a vaudeville house that would later be known as the Palace Theatre. This facility was designed by Thomas Lamb of New York, who also designed the Ohio Theatre on Capitol Square, constructed two years after the Palace. The Ohio Theatre is considered the finest Golden Age movie palace in the state and is recognized as the "Official Theatre of the State of Ohio." The terra-cotta facade of the building is dominated by a Corinthian distyle-in-muris porch set between bays defined by coupled Corinthian pilasters at each edge. The auditorium was immense—over 3,000 seats—but completely free of interior supports, so the sightlines are unobstructed.[21]

The success of the Leveque Tower convinced the city fathers of Columbus that investment in the city's riverfront could work. Columbus revised its plans for a civic center and moved its city hall to the west side of Front Street, directly across the street from the LeVeque itself. At the same time, the state government realized that there was no more room in the Statehouse for Ohio's growing government. In 1929, the legislature passed a bill allowing for a temporary property tax to pay for a new state office building located on the Scioto River west of the capitol. It was imagined that a set of state buildings would occupy the blocks between the Broad Street Bridge and Town Street.

The architect chosen to design the Ohio State Office Building (1929–35; now the Ohio Judicial Center) was Harry Hake from Cincinnati (fig. 18). Hake's design for the building was fundamentally classical, particularly in its form and its fusion of the fine and decorative arts into the building. The building's massing was suggested by its site: a twelve-story slab, just seven bays deep but thirty-six bays wide, rests on a two-story base. Although the building is constructed of steel and concrete, a cladding of Georgia marble was used for consistency with its new neighbors in the emerging Columbus civic center. The classical details are limited and stylized. Doric columns serve as an inset colonnade at the ends of the eleventh and twelfth floors, and suggestions of pilasters and a Doric entablature are present at the "corps de logis" at the center of the building.

POST-WORLD WAR II DISINVESTMENT AND RENEWAL

Columbus grew into a major metropolis in the decades after World War II, but this development occurred around Ohio State University and beyond the inner-ring suburbs. The second half of the twentieth century was not as kind to Ohio as a whole. As other states in the West and the Sunbelt drew population and jobs away from the Midwest with a warmer climate and right-to-work laws, Ohio's cities began to hollow out from the inside. Cincinnati, hampered by its inability to incorporate its metropolitan territory, lost 40 percent of its population between 1950 and 2000. Cleveland lost over 50 percent. Some smaller cities, such as Youngstown, suffered even greater losses.

It has been essential that Ohio's cities leverage the resources they still have to stabilize and eventually grow their economies. A primary tool to that end has been the employment of the federal and, later, state tax credits for historic preservation. Ohio ranks as the number-one user of the federal tax credits by number of projects, and number two in the dollar value of those projects. Since the federal credit began, over 2,500 Ohio buildings have qualified, representing over $7.5 billion of construction, and an investment of $1.5 billion in credits. At the state level, nearly 700 projects have been approved since 2008 through a competitive process, and these have earned an additional $1 billion in state credits.[22]

Many of the buildings highlighted in this essay have been or are being rehabilitated using the tax credits, either directly or in conjunction with private financing. For example, the residential conversion of Terminal Tower, the Leveque Tower, and Carew Tower have all been made possible by the combined federal and state tax credits. The credits, too, have made space available for nonprofits and arts programs—both the Dayton Arcade project and the renovations of the Palace and Capitol Theatres in Columbus relied on the federal tax credit as a key component of their financing.

As Ohio looks to its future, it cannot help but appreciate its past. While the manufacturing economy that rocketed the state to political power in the nineteenth century is unlikely to return to anything near what it had been, the state has many other assets it can leverage for success in the future. Among these are Ohio's

Fig. 18. Ohio State Office Building (now Ohio Judicial Center), Columbus, by Harry Hake, 1930–33.

historic building stock and its wide range of livable communities, legacies of the state's boom years over a century ago.

Jeffrey Tilman is Associate Director of the School of Architecture and Interior Design at the University of Cincinnati. He teaches courses on architectural history and composition and historic preservation. Tilman's research focuses on American architecture between the Civil War and World War II. His book, *Arthur Brown, Jr.: Progressive Classicist*, remains the principal source for information on the San Francisco-based architect. He is a licensed architect in his native state of California but has called Ohio home for the last twenty-five years.

Notes

1. Daniel R. Porter, "Collections and Exhibits: The Rufus Putnam House at the Campus Martius Museum," *Ohio History* 73, 183–87. The Putnam House is open for tours as part of the Campus Martius Museum.

2. All census and population data comes from the Community Research Partners' "Data Byte 5: Census 1810–2010: Celebrating 200 Years of the Census in Ohio," issued in March 2010, https://www.issuelab.org/resources/3973/3973.pdf, accessed March 30, 2025.

3. *An Act to enable the People of the Eastern division of the territory Northwest of the river Ohio to form a Constitution and State Government*, April 30, 1802. General Records of the United States Government, 7th Congress, 1st Session, 2 Statute 173, Chapter 40, Record Group 11. This act led to a constitutional convention, which was held on November 1, 1802, at Chillicothe. The state's constitution was ratified by the people on November 27, 1802. United States National Archives, "200th Anniversary of Ohio Statehood," https://www.archives.gov/legislative/features/ohio-statehood, accessed May 29, 2025.

4. Michael W. Fazio and Patrick Snadon, *The Domestic Architecture of Benjamin Henry Latrobe* (Baltimore: Johns Hopkins University Press, 2006), 301-14.

5. Worthington's first Senate term, from 1803 to 1807, was an initial four-year term. Worthington later succeeded Return J. Meigs, who resigned to become governor, in the other senate seat, and completed that term between 1810 and 1814, at which time Worthington replaced Meigs as governor. .

6. The population continued to grow at a steady rate year after year until 1950, at which time it peaked at just over 500,000 inhabitants.

7. A renovation in the 1990s revealed a suite of landscape murals by Robert Seldon Duncanson, an African American painter of the Hudson River School. Commissioned by Nicholas Longworth in 1850, the murals were restored by the museum and are now featured works in the collection.

8. So termed by the *London Illustrated Gazette*, May 1850. Reported by Blanche Linden, "From Inns to Hotels in Cincinnati," www.hillforest.org. Quoted in James O'Gorman, *Isaiah Rogers: Architectural Practice in Antebellum America* (Boston: University of Massachusetts Press, 2015), 149. In 1850, Rogers was asked to design a replacement for the recently burned Hamilton County Courthouse and Jail. Rogers eventually superintended the construction of a three-story Greek Revival building, but the design was from the office of Walter & Wilson, one of the architects of the Statehouse. For Rogers's early work in Cincinnati, see O'Gorman, *Isaiah Rogers*, 143-76.

9. An extensive renovation in the 1950s, designed by Edward J. Schulte, extended the chancel of the church and added transepts. A great deal of gilding and a suite of marbles were used in the interior to create a sumptuous and dramatic effect that suggests where Art Deco design might have gone had the World War II not altered the course of design history.

10. The elevations of the two buildings are identical. This history was told to me by my former colleague Gerald Larson, who will publish more detail in his upcoming book on the buildings of Chicago. He discusses the interior atrium of the Shillito's building on his blog, *The Architecture Professor,* https://thearchitectureprofessor.com/2020/06/29/6-14-the-use-of-iron-framing-in-shillitos/, accessed July 6, 2025.

11. Gerald Larson, "Ingalls Building," *Archipedia*, https://sah-archipedia.org/buildings/OH-01-061-0054, accessed July 6, 2025.

12. Jeffrey T. Darbee, "Cincinnati Museum Center," *Archipedia*, https://sah-archipedia.org/buildings/OH-01-061-0073, accessed July 6, 2025.

13. Darwin H. Stapleton (of the Rockefeller Archive Center), "Industry," *Encyclopedia of Cleveland History*, Case Western Reserve University, www.case.edu/ech/articles/i/industry, accessed June 27, 2025. It would take until 1911 for the Oil Trusts to be broken up by United States Supreme Court.

14. Ernest G. Spittler. "Chemical Industry," *Encyclopedia of Cleveland History*, Case Western Reserve University, www.case.edu/ech/articles/c/ichemical-industry, accessed June 27, 2025.

15. Mary-Peale Schofield, "The Cleveland Arcade," *Journal of the Society of Architectural Historians* 25, no. 4 (1966): 281-91.

16. "Museum History," https://www.clevelandart.org/about-museum/museum-history, accessed June 28, 2025.

17. The National Cash Register Corporation transferred the house to the Wright Family Foundation in 2006, and in turn the house was gifted to Historic Dayton, which now operates the house as a museum.

18. Evan Millward, "Cincinnatians Lend Expertise to 'Most Transformative Project in America," WCPO News, March 23, 2021, transcript, https://www.wcpo.com/news/transportation-development/move-up-cincinnati/cincinnatians-lend-expertise-to-most-transformative-project-in-america, accessed July 3, 2025.

19. The first state capitol was in Chillicothe. Between 1810 and 1812, the legislature met in Zanesville while a more permanent site could be identified.

20. Kniffen first uses the term in "Louisiana House Types," *Annals of the Association of American Geographers* 26 (1936).

21. The stage, fly, and back-of-house facilities were completely rebuilt in the early 1970s by the Columbus Association for the Performing Arts, and it is now primarily a venue for touring Broadway shows and concerts.

22. All statistics on Ohio's historic tax credits courtesy of Mariangela Pfister, Department Head and Deputy State Historic Preservation Officer for Technical Preservation Services, Ohio State Historic Preservation Office, Columbus Ohio. E-mail sent June 30, 2025.

OHIO'S CLASSICAL RENAISSANCE

RULE AND INVENTION IN THE FEDERAL AND GRECIAN ERA

WILLIAM HEYER

"There are two ways by which a people can imitate the style of architecture of another country; the one true, and the other false. The true mode is less an imitation than an adoption and consists in receiving as an alphabet in their entire shape the system, the rules, and the taste of a style of architecture. It was thus that the Romans adopted the architecture of the Greeks . . . . It was thus also with the nations of modern Europe, who, abandoning the Gothic and the incongruities of the Middle Ages, have appropriated the Greek and Roman styles by legitimate adoption."

—James Elmes, *Dictionary of the Fine Arts*, 1826

The architecture of the Italian Renaissance was an expression of the glory of ancient Rome in its emulation of monuments, temples, and villas and a firm establishment of Vitruvian rules following the late Middle Ages. Inventiveness and *eurythmia* filled the minds of Renaissance architects who borrowed from the past but applied the classic rules in new ways. Early to mid-nineteenth-century American architects likewise revived classical learning and applied the Roman and Greek vocabulary with a distinctly American slant in their built works and new pattern books based on Renaissance and eighteenth-century treatises. This enterprise was especially active in Ohio, where architects, builders, and patrons, armed with pattern books and an increasingly sophisticated understanding of architectural history, contributed significantly to the classical revival.[1] In this joint participation of the citizenry in developing new architecture, Ohio imitated the Italian Renaissance as an ideal.

Fig. 1. Atwood-Wilson House, Chillicothe, built by Jacob S. Atwood, 1845.

FORMULATING AN IDEAL ARCHITECTURE IN THE EARLY NINETEENTH CENTURY

Ohio builders and their patrons absorbed and developed modern architectural principles in a short period of time, from roughly 1810 to 1850. This agility originated with a nascent American freedom, "virgin land," and the prospect of wealth and peace, particularly after the War of 1812. Notably, this classical momentum was nurtured in the prospect that America could establish its own identity, set its own course, and do so with a fresh and free eye to both the future and the past. Ohio and the Northwest Territory were growing with an array of peoples and cultures from the former colonies and abroad. They comprised a new middle class that was well traveled, well educated, and with a reputation to prove to their European predecessors. They prided themselves on their new democratic republic, often harkening back to ancient Rome and Greece in their tastes and values. In a sense, an Ohio farmer living in his Grecian house on his own farm was seen as a classical symbol of the integrity, autonomy, and eternal essence of the human person.[2]

In the early nineteenth century, Ohio architecture was maturing and emulating the ancients in striking ways. This classical fervor was bolstered by architects who brought their talents to new towns of the "hinterland" far beyond the Eastern Seaboard. William Strickland left Philadelphia and settled in Nashville in 1845; James and Charles Dakin and James Gallier all left New York for

Photo: William Heyer

Photo: Greg Hume, CC BY-SA 3.0

Fig. 2. Cathedral Basilica of St. Peter in Chains, Cincinnati, by Henry Walter, 1841-45.

Photo: Shim Harno/Alamy Stock Photo

Fig. 3. Kirtland Temple, construction directed by Joseph Smith, 1836.

New Orleans circa 1835; Francis Costigan of Baltimore for Indiana in 1837; and Isaiah Rogers of Boston for Cincinnati in the 1840s. These architects brought to the frontier a classical authority in theory and practice. Other prominent architects remained in their eastern offices and developed sophisticated pattern books (notably, Minard Lafever and Asher Benjamin), while the regional builders and patrons collaborated with them and absorbed these pattern books with zeal. By the 1830s, Ohio was an important workshop for classicism.[3]

Early nineteenth-century architecture in Ohio was at first Federal, developed from the popular dialect of Scotsmen Robert and James Adam (the "Adamesque" or "Adam" style). Later fusions and transformations of Federal and Grecian forms revealed a maturing classicism, lively and inventive, borrowing without prejudice from both Roman and Greek precedent. A truly modern architecture with strength, vitality, and elegance appeared even through hybridizations and diverse interpretations.

One example is the Willard Warner House in Granville, Ohio (1815; fig. 4). Built of local red brick in Flemish bond pattern, the details on this standard Federal mass blossom with Adamesque flair. The window brickmolds are thin, grouped colonettes joined at corner rosettes. The frieze is a wily line of swags and ovals drawing the eye upward and across to unique metal "Ionic" leader boxes atop the downspouts. The frontispiece recalls Federal and Adamesque decorative mirror frames with its rows of small soffit globes, while the plancier projects like an overmantel and curves slightly outward to protect arriving guests from the rain and snow. The combination of these decorative elements is far beyond the staid elevations of other Federal domestic architecture and serves as a creative opening salvo for the new architecture of Ohio.

CLASSICAL REVIVAL IN THE MID-NINETEENTH CENTURY

Following the Federal period, a so-called "Classic Revival" of interesting and mildly clumsy temple houses emerged.[4] The 1835 Sturges-Kennan-Fulstow House in Norwalk by William Meade, with its odd elongated octagonal piers, and the 1820 Baum-Taft house in Cincinnati (see p. 9 in this volume) by an unknown designer, with its attenuated paired columns, are examples. Jonathan Goldsmith constructed several of these "stretched" temples in the Western Reserve in the

Photo: William Heyer

Fig. 4. Willard Warner House, Granville, built 1815.

1820s. Short-lived, this development would be followed by a transition to a mature classical architecture in the 1830s and '40s, thanks to talented architects, Grecian pattern books, and sophisticated builders and patrons.

Attempts at classical imitation abound in this transition. Among them are the Renick-Young House (Mount Oval), built by William Renick near Circleville (1832), with its James Gibbs–inspired floor plan of recessed porticoes and corner bays, and the Atwood-Wilson House, built by Jacob S. Atwood in Chillicothe (1845), with its finely carved stone Tower of the Winds columns and an entablature featuring what can only be described as "carpenter" quartered mutules (fig. 1). Other examples include an unnamed, undated house near Seville with a frontispiece featuring a single Ionic column rent in two making way for the door, and a one-story unnamed, undated temple house near Wellington showcasing a full-length portico inspired by the less-imitated Choragic monument of Thrasyllus. All these present a remarkable and inventive use of Roman and Greek forms in the domestic architecture of Ohio.

GRECIAN INFLUENCE AND INVENTION IN ECCLESIASTICAL BUILDINGS

In their early attempts at emulation and invention, Ohio builders frequently melded Federal, Gothic, and Grecian forms, notably in ecclesiastical architecture. The Congregational-Presbyterian Church in Kinsman (1831), designed and built by Willie Smith from Asher Benjamin's Federal pattern book *The American Builder's Companion*, bears an entablature with triglyphs spaced every other mutule, but misaligned with the pointed Gothic windows below. The mutules are the most canonical detail on the church. The Congregational Church at Claridon (1831) borrows pilasters and an entablature from Asher Benjamin's *The Architect, or Practical House Carpenter*, 1830 (pl. 28; fig. 11), to form a double entry like a schoolhouse. The Masonic Temple in Lancaster (1845) is a Greek temple in form, with an entry frontispiece below the socle modeled on the Choragic Monument of Thrasyllus; yet it has large, pointed Gothic windows between Grecian pilasters on all sides of the two-story

Photo: William Heyer

Fig. 5. Bartlett-Cunningham-Gerber House, Chillicothe, built 1855.

lodge room. The Mormon temple at Kirtland (1836; fig. 3) likewise combines a temple form and Adamesque details with pointed Gothic windows.

In ensuing mature ecclesiastical designs, builders finally produced unified Grecian compositions rather than hybrid arrangements. The Presbyterian Female Seminary (1847, later the Wooster-Boalt House) in Norwalk, 60 miles southwest of Cleveland, is a sophisticated modern design with an Ionic *distylos in antis* portico. The articulation of the facade is directly from Benjamin's *The Architect, or Complete Builder's Guide*, including the window surrounds. The architect and builder are unknown but the extant form indicates that pattern books assisted in the harmonious composition of the whole with its individual parts.

The Cathedral of St. Peter in Chains in Cincinnati (1845; fig. 2), now a basilica, was designed by Henry Walter, the award-winning architect of the new state capitol in Columbus. Made of Ohio limestone, St. Peter's features a central octagonal spire proclaiming Walter's skill at emulating the English spires of James Gibbs and William Inwood. Lafever and Benjamin delineated similar spires in their pattern books. The *prostylos hexastylos* semi-peripteral portico with Tower of the Winds columns rises over 33 feet from an elevated stylobate twenty steps above street level, making this the tallest church in the city and west of the Appalachians at completion.[5] The proportions and fine details reveal the sophistication of Walter, who was formerly a partner of Alexander Jackson Davis.

OHIO'S GRECIAN TEMPLE HOUSES

Ohio's classical refinement in the mid-nineteenth century shines most brightly in its domestic architecture. The 1842 Alfred Avery house in Granville (1842, also known as Avery-Downer House, now the Robbins Hunter Museum; fig. 6), 34 miles northeast of Columbus, stands today as one of America's finest wood-framed Grecian temple houses. Palladian in overall arrangement, its *tetrastylos prostylos* two-story portico with Ilissos Ionic columns is inspired by plate 75 in Lafever's *Modern Builder's Guide*. The Doric wings of the house imitate the temple of Theseus, and the entry frontispiece, inspired by Lafever's published designs, combines the entablature of the Choragic Monument of Thrasyllus with columns of the Tower of the Winds. At once Doric, Ionic, and Corinthian, the Avery house is a model of modern Grecian architecture.

In 1825, when construction commenced on the Ohio and Erie Canal, Alfred Avery owned a near majority of stock, including the canal extension from Cleveland to Newark near Granville. Not long after, another Alfred (Kelley), first mayor of Cleveland, state representative, and the genius behind Ohio's canal system, began planning for his stately home near the rising capitol in Columbus. Kelley and Avery likely met on occasion to review the ongoing operations of the canal system and shared a common interest in architecture. Alfred Avery was just starting a building campaign for St Luke's Episcopal Church in Granville and needed an architect and a high-quality builder. Benjamin Morgan, a reputable mason and craftsman who later worked on the state capitol, accepted Avery's invitation to build St Luke's and, subsequently, Avery's wood-framed temple house. Morgan was also

Photo: Christopher Riley

Fig. 6. Avery-Downer House (now Robbins Hunter Museum), Granville, by Benjamin Morgan, 1842.

likely the mason for the Alfred Kelley House (1836–38).

Kelley's mansion was built entirely of Berea sandstone. It featured three Ilissos Ionic two-story porches *in antis* on the north, west, and east facades and one Ilissos Ionic two-story *prostylos* portico at the entry facing Broad Street. It was demolished in 1961.

All records indicate that Kelley was his own architect. But this sophisticated design is more likely from the hand of a well-trained architect. The centralized plan with porches *in antis* was uncommon and only found somewhat similarly delineated in James Gibbs's 1728 *Book of Architecture*. It was not utilized in domestic architecture in the United States in the eighteenth or nineteenth centuries, except at Mount Oval (previously mentioned) and one house near Cincinnati attributed to gentleman builder Thomas Carneal.[6] Minard Lafever, then at a high point in his career, certainly would have been familiar with Gibbs's plan. And Abbott Lowell Cummings, in his brief history of Alfred Kelley and the Kelley house, implies that Minard Lafever did influence the design.[7]

It is notable that the Alfred Avery House and the Alfred Kelley House present similar themes: the Kelley house with a two-story Ilissos Ionic temple portico in sandstone; the Avery house with the same but in wood. The Kelley house incorporated a centralized floor plan found only in obscure classical precedent; the Avery house uniquely married every Grecian order. Together these designs point to the sophistication and creativity of Minard Lafever.

ONE-STORY TEMPLE HOUSES

Situated forty-eight miles south of Columbus in Chillicothe, Ohio's first capital, is the one-story brick Bartlett-Cunningham-Gerber House (1855; fig. 5). The one-story format, a transplant from Virginia, was common in the southern half of Ohio in the early to mid-nineteenth century. This house presents an inventive and refined use of Grecian forms. The portico entablature is supported by wood Tower of the Winds columns with brick antae. Above, the parapet decoration employs a well-ordered combination of forms derived from pattern books. The door and window lintels in the portico are inspired by Lafever's *Beauties of Modern Architecture* (pls. 6 and 19), while inside, the

Photo: William Heyer

Fig. 7. Edmiston Wilder House, West Andover, built by Leverett Osborn, 1845.

door casings and window surrounds are similar to plates 31 and 32 in Asher Benjamin's *The Architect, or, Complete Builder's Guide*. A unified "Corinthian" design, the Bartlett-Cunningham-Gerber House stands as Ohio's preeminent Grecian one-story temple house.

In Brownhelm, near Vermilion, 40 miles west of Cleveland, lie the foundations of the Joseph Swift House (1840). It was lost to a fire in the 1920s, and photographs and drawings are all that survive (Frary pls. 91–93, 147).[8] The form is remarkable, as a one-story wood-framed farmhouse with an imaginative extended Ilissos Ionic portico *in antis* bookended with "French Room" parlors where the best furniture would have been customarily displayed. The exterior window surrounds at these parlors are similar to those delineated by Minard Lafever in *The Beauties of Modern Architecture* and appearing at the Bartlett-Cunningham-Gerber House in Chillicothe. As Swift was originally from western Massachusetts, he, like Avery and Kelley, would have known the buildings and pattern books of Lafever and quite possibly called on him to design his new home. A learned man and successful farmer, Joseph Swift exemplified the agrarian and classical ideals that he honored in the design of his Grecian temple house.

MID-NINETEENTH-CENTURY INNOVATIONS

Two uniquely innovative structures from the middle of the nineteenth century in Ohio are the George Hatch House in Cincinnati and the Edmiston Wilder House in West Andover.

Isaiah Rogers, newly settled in Cincinnati, designed a traditional Boston row house in limestone for George Hatch in 1851. What makes this house remarkable is the curious central portico framed by the bows. A late example of innovation in Grecian architecture, the portico is a wall-less Tower of the Winds; semi-octagonal with attenuated Athenian details continuing up into the enclosed second floor, and a stunted dome above the entry door. The house interior is decorated with Corinthian pilasters and delicately detailed lintels akin to those in Lafever's *Beauties of Modern Architecture*. Although Rogers was primarily involved in public architecture throughout his career, his domestic designs were sophisticated and unique, from the Captain Robert Bennet Forbes House (1834) in Milton, Massachusetts, to the eccentric Hillforest (1855) in Aurora, Indiana. It is hard to imagine from his hands, however, a more overtly Grecian and inventive design so unified both inside and out, than the George Hatch House.

Along Ohio's northeastern border with Pennsylvania, among sporadic surviving Grecian structures, stands the Edmiston Wilder House (1845) in West Andover built by Leverett Osborn (fig. 7). Osborn, originally from the Connecticut Valley, constructed this house in Palladian form with Grecian detail. The Doric entablature continuously wraps the first floor (three sides) and projects slightly at the *in-antis* entry portico. The second-floor portico is curiously Ionic with capital-less and base-less fluted columns.[9] Osborn relied for the most part on Asher Benjamin's *The Practice of Architecture* and followed the Doric details strictly. But he veered from canon for some difficult conditions like the sloped "roof" of the entry portico, which forced an unusual top-clipped triglyph on the return of the entablature. He also incorporated Benjamin's invented option for bases at the entry's Greek Doric columns. The pilasters beautifully articulate the facade inside of which appear convex fluted piers—a detail not found in Benjamin.

OHIO'S TIMELESS CLASSICISM

The development of modern classicism by leading architects and regional builders in Ohio of the early to mid-nineteenth century cannot be found elsewhere. It was here and then that there existed no in situ Georgian or Neoclassical precedent, thereby providing the freedom for architects, builders and patrons to both imitate and invent. Ohio's new architecture was totally American in complete fusion with its ideals, thoroughly modern, based on the ancients, and developed with great sophistication. Like the creative architecture of the Italian Renaissance just a few centuries before, it exudes monumentality, identity, and a rejuvenation of Vitruvian principles developed with "lively mental energy."[10] Ohio's architecture of the Federal and Grecian era presents us with a model of innovative yet timeless classicism.

Notably, several American alumni of the École des Beaux-Arts, which continued classical instruction based on Greek and Roman models for the remainder of the nineteenth century, graced Ohio with work reflecting their training. These include Charles McKim, James Gamble Rogers, and John Russell Pope.[11] And, although Victorian and Modernist sensibilities prevailed for a time, there can be no doubt that the creativity and potency of this nineteenth century renaissance in young Ohio nurtured a tradition that continues to be reborn.

William Heyer is an architect in Columbus and co-founder of the Ohio & Lake Erie Chapter of the Institute of Classical Architecture & Art.

Notes

1. On the use of pattern books, see Daniel D. Reiff, *Houses from Books: Treatises, Pattern Books, and Catalogs in American Architecture, 1738–1950: A History and Guide* (University Park, PA: Pennsylvania State University Press, 2001).

2. Talbot Hamlin, chap. 12, "Why the Greek Revival Flourished," in *Greek Revival Architecture in America* (New York: Dover, 1964), 326–29.

3. Hamlin, *Greek Revival Architecture*. See also chap. 1, pt. 1, "The New Classicism," and chap. 11, "Westward Ways," p. 280, for context.

4. See I. T. Frary, *Early Homes of Ohio* (Richmond, VA: Garrett & Massie, 1936), chapter on the Classic Revival (pp. 47–61), and Virginia and Lee McAlester, *A Field Guide to American Houses* (New York: Alfred A. Knopf, 1997; originally published 1984), chapter on Early Classical Revival (pp. 169–75).

5. Jeff Suess, "Our History: Storied cathedral noted for its architecture," *Cincinnati Enquirer*, August 18, 2017 (updated), https://www.cincinnati.com/story/news/2017/07/26/our-history-storied-cathedral-noted-its-architecture/512371001/s architecture.

6. The Carneal-designed house is Elmwood Hall in Ludlow, Kentucky. This house has sometimes been attributed to Benjamin Latrobe and is singular for its use of recessed porticoes on two sides (one now enclosed) with a domed entry salon. See Historic American Buildings Survey, Elmwood Hall, 246 Forest Avenue, Ludlow, Kenton County, KY, 1933, https://www.loc.gov/item/ky0079/, Library of Congress, Photographs & Prints Division. Nowhere is the Gibbs plan used verbatim, but the Kelley house plan with three recessed porticoes indicates definitive use.

7. Abbott Lowell Cummings, *The Alfred Kelley House of Columbus, Ohio* (Columbus, OH: Franklin County Historical Society, 1953), 9, 11, 13.

8. See Frary, *Early Homes of Ohio*, pt. 4, "Dwellings," pp. 16–63. Illustrations of the Swift House are found throughout the book.

9. Thomas Gordon Smith, introduction to *Practice of Architecture; The Builder's Guide: Two Pattern Books of American Classical Architecture* by Asher Benjamin (New York: Da Capo Press, repr. 1994), xiv, xv. It is Smith's opinion that the second-floor portico was a later addition.

10 The term "lively mental energy" (*vigore mobile*; Vitruvius, *On Architecture*, Book I, II, 2) is central to a classical understanding of invention under the rule *dispositio*. Thomas Gordon Smith (1948–2021), in the introduction to his book *Vitruvius on Architecture* (New York: The Monacelli Press, 2003, 19), calls out this important detail and used the term in his classes, lectures, and writings to inspire and motivate a generation of young classicists.

11. McKim, Mead & White at the National McKinley Birthplace Memorial (Niles) and the Butler Institute of American Art (Youngstown); Rogers at Laurel Court (Cincinnati); and Pope at the First Congregational Church (Columbus) and the Cincinnati Gas & Electric Company Building.

1876

THE CLASSICAL COUNTY COURTHOUSES OF OHIO

BARBARA POWERS

The surveyors are gone, the pioneers are gone, the land remains. In the years that have followed the recording of the first deeds, the deed books have been transferred from courthouse to courthouse to serve as the ultimate authority . . . to the ownership of the land . . . a town like ours would have no excuse for being were it not the county seat; the courthouse justifies its existence.
— Helen Hooven Santmyer, *Ohio Town*, 1962

Ohio's county courthouses stand as symbols of economic aspirations, civic ideals, and local pride, telling the story of Ohio. Their designs reflect a sequence of classical architectural statements, reinforce national stylistic trends, define local architectural character, and comprise the work of important architects within the state. These courthouses serve as architectural declamations of Ohio's development as a state of national stature.

Practically speaking, county courthouses house the judicial, administrative, and legislative functions of government. As a public building type, their primary purpose is to provide facilities for court functions with the courtroom, the most prominent space. As county government's responsibilities grew, courthouses developed into the center of county business, with spaces to register land transactions, births, and deaths; collect taxes; and provide for public assembly. As symbols of justice, law and order, and the establishment of rights, county courthouses are conspicuously situated on public squares defining the town center of county seats.

Courthouses became the centerpiece of the county seat, with their location as integral to their prominence as their architecture. The courthouse square served as the hub of business, political, and social activities. Midwestern county seats typically feature courthouse squares of rectangular blocks surrounded by streets, with the courthouse, the most monumental, ornate building in the county, standing in the center of the square, and business blocks surrounding the square on all four sides. Most of Ohio's county seats were laid out by a surveyor who platted the streets and a promoter focused on selling lots and seeing the town grow. The courthouse square served as the nucleus of the county seat, which often became the largest town and trade center in the county.

Fig 1. Licking County Courthouse, Newark, by Henry E. Myer 1876–78.

Photo: Andre Jenny/Alamy Stock Photo

Early courthouse building types and styles can be traced through the migration of settlers from the eastern United States. Likewise, the configuration of courthouse squares reflects the influence of the New England public green, market squares of Virginia, and public squares in Pennsylvanian towns familiar to the settlers coming into Ohio.

Ohio's courthouse architecture shows a progression of classical design that can be divided into four phases. From 1800 to 1850, the foursquare courthouse type and Greek Revival style predominated; the decades from 1850 to 1880 were characterized by Picturesque Italianate and Second Empire styles. The golden age of Ohio courthouses—in which formally trained architects drew upon Beaux-Arts classicism and Renaissance Revival along with the influence of Henry Hobson Richardson's Romanesque—occurred from 1880 to 1930; and from 1930 to 1970, federal programs and post–World War II growth and change created modern blends of classicism, from "stripped" classicism to New Formalism.

1800–50: FOURSQUARE COURTHOUSES AND GREEK REVIVAL TEMPLES OF JUSTICE

Established as a state in 1803, Ohio witnessed its first period of permanent courthouse architecture in the early nineteenth century. Ohio's first constitution divided the state into three judicial circuits, each with a judge of the court and three associate judges.[1] Nascent statehood and settlement from roughly 1800 to 1850 includes courthouse forms and styles reflecting the influence of settlers from New England, the Mid-Atlantic states, and Virginia. Ohio's earliest courthouses are marked by classical design rooted in knowledge of the antiquities gained from builders' guides, pattern books, and practical planning through two distinct forms: the foursquare and temple-front types.

The foursquare type, an American vernacular building form, migrated westward as a prototype for many of the earliest county courthouses in the states comprising the Northwest Territory. Between 1800 and 1835, an estimated thirty Ohio counties built foursquare type courthouses.[2] These courthouses were concentrated in the center of the eastern portion of the state and scattered across its southern two-thirds. This pattern links the foursquare building type to predominant settlement patterns defining early Ohio, marked by migration from the eastern United States. The foursquare type was likely derived from English meeting houses or town halls and sprang up as meeting houses, churches, town halls, schools, and courthouses throughout the eastern states during the late eighteenth and early nineteenth centuries. Relocating New Englanders attempted to recreate the meeting houses of their former towns in their new home, and Ohio settlers from the states of Pennsylvania, Delaware, New Jersey, and Virginia replicated the foursquare form in their most important public building, the county courthouse.[3]

While the 1820 Meigs County Courthouse in Chester (now a museum of the Meigs County Historical Society) is the oldest remaining Ohio county courthouse, the 1829 original Perry County Courthouse (now a town hall) in Somerset in southwestern Ohio holds the claim as the state's oldest building of the foursquare type in continuous government use since its construction. Built from plans by James Hampson, Esq., the two-story building has a typical square-shaped form and a low-pitched hipped roof topped by a spire (fig. 2).[4]

Photo: Christopher Riley

Fig. 2. Old Perry County Courthouse, Somerset, plans by James Hampson, Esq., 1828–29.

In the southwestern part of the state, the Old Montgomery County Courthouse in Dayton offers an outstanding example of Greek Revival architecture (fig. 4). Constructed in 1847–50 and designed by Cincinnati architect Howard Daniels, the Greek temple-front limestone courthouse features Ionic columns and pilasters, a coffered-ceiling portico, pediment, simple entablature with dentils, and stone-shingled gable roof. At the rear of the building, freestanding columns at each corner flank four Ionic pilasters in antis, giving the illusion of an open portico similar to the facade.

Daniels's plan for the Dayton courthouse incorporates practical design aspects to create a workable, efficient interior space. The elliptical courtroom with domed coffered ceiling is the dominant space, and a grand spiral staircase provides the main public access to the courtroom, with secondary circulation patterns allowing for the separation of judge, jury, and defendant entering the courtroom.[5]

The public concern for building a "safe, permanent, and durable Courthouse"[6] is reflected in the architect's focus on fireproof design and construction. The Grecian stylistic emphasis and the fireproof construction techniques suggest the possible influences of Robert Mills's Treasury Building in Washington, DC, completed in 1842, with the overall temple form resembling the Connecticut State Capitol by Ithiel Town from 1827.

At the time of its completion, the Montgomery County Courthouse was described as "the most elegant and costly building of its kind in Ohio."[7] Such boosterism was commonplace, demonstrating the competition between counties to capitalize on the success of their county courthouse to further the growth and prosperity of their county seat.

Variations of the Greek Revival temple-front model are seen in courthouses constructed in Highland, Meigs, Brown, and Knox Counties. The 1832–35 Highland County courthouse in Hillsboro features Ionic pilasters supporting arches over the window bays, presenting an interesting arcade detail. Pomeroy, the second Meigs county seat, provides a hilltop location overlooking the Ohio River for the 1845–48 temple-front courthouse with a two-story in-antis entrance and twin circular stairs. The 1849–51 Brown and the later 1854–56 Knox courthouses are similar in their overall Greek Revival design; both display recessed entrances flanked by freestanding columns topped by a pediment and entablature and cupola (fig. 3). These temple-form expressions of the Greek Revival show the style in its symbolic imagery, not as replicas of antiquity, but through the common language of classical forms and details clearly standing as a statement of nationally recognizable public governmental architecture.

Photo: Christopher Riley

Fig. 3. Knox County Courthouse, Mount Vernon, by Hubbard Baker, 1854–56.

1850–80: PICTURESQUE ITALIANATE AND SECOND EMPIRE COURTHOUSES

Mid-nineteenth-century county courthouses demonstrate the rapid development of Ohio from a frontier settlement of traveling circuit judges to highly organized county governments with multiple courts and specialized departments created to address the needs of the growing population. The 1851 Ohio constitutional amendments eliminated the earlier three-judicial-circuit system by creating nine judicial districts, each with three subdivisions with an elected Common Pleas Judge. The courthouse became the center of county government, and the building's interior spaces expanded to include its judicial and administrative functions.[8]

During the period leading up to and immediately following the Civil War, Ohio was emblematic of the swiftly growing nation. Newly constructed county courthouses conveyed the full confidence and optimism of the era.

Photo: Ilene MacDonald/Alamy Stock Photo

Fig. 4. Old Montgomery County Courthouse, Dayton, by Howard Daniels, 1847–50.

Photo: Christopher Riley

Fig 5. Ross County Courthouse, Chillicothe, by Collins & Autenrieth, 1855–58.

As Ohio's county seats matured, the earlier courthouses were replaced by larger buildings reflecting mid- to late nineteenth-century styles, including Second Empire, Italianate, and, later, Richardsonian Romanesque, Beaux-Arts, Renaissance Revival, and Neoclassicism.

Ohio's courthouse architecture during the 1850s–80s transitions from Greek Revival interpretations to the picturesque historicism of the Italianate and Second Empire styles. Examples from this period display subdued designs melding with the previous temple-front models evolving into grander, more exuberant expressions, leading into Gilded Age opulence. Mid-nineteenth-century courthouses also show the growing professionalism of architects.

Typical characteristics of the Italianate style include projecting cornices with ornately carved brackets, tall, relatively narrow windows with carved hoodmolds, more decorative treatment overall, and tall clock towers. Located in Chillicothe, Ohio's first state capitol, the 1855–58 Ross County Courthouse shows a transition between the temple-front form and Italianate, featuring a two-story temple-front entrance with pediment topped by a clock tower (fig. 5). Flanking the entrance, the courthouse plan stretches out on both sides with separate entrance bays, each with carved lettering calling out the various county offices of clerk, sheriff, and probate judge to the left, and recorder, treasurer, and auditor to the right—the most architecturally distinctive evidence of nineteenth-century growth of county government. The 1869–70 red-brick Geauga County Courthouse, at the north end of a tree-lined public square in the town of Chardon, is a distinctive example of the Italianate style. The projecting three-story main entrance tower is topped by a tall hexagonal clock tower that can be seen from a distance coming into town.

Second Empire–style courthouses are characterized by a mansard roof and a profusion of ornamentation and monumentality. Rising upon the flat landscape that defines northwest Ohio, the 1874–76 Van Wert County Courthouse makes a grand statement in downtown Van Wert with its red brick, stone quoins and ornate window trim, and complex mansard roof featuring corner towers dominated by the tall center clock tower. The Muskingum County and Licking County courthouses, located in Zanesville and Newark, respectively, display the highly ornate Second Empire style of architect Henry E. Myer, who designed several mid-nineteenth-century Ohio courthouses (see fig. 1). Commanding the center of the town's public square, these examples are designed to be seen from all sides with similar details and entrances on all elevations topped by lively roofs with corner towers and a central clock tower. This courthouse model carried forward into the late nineteenth and early twentieth centuries.

State legislation passed in 1869 furthered the construction of public buildings at the county level. It allowed county commissioners to issue bonds to raise funds for public buildings and levy taxes for seven years to pay off interest and a portion of the principal. Importantly, the legislation distinguished between trained architects and carpenters or builders by requiring the plans be drawn and the project supervised by professional architects.[9]

The 1870s also saw the development of the jail and sheriff's residence building type, representing another distinctive Midwestern form shaping the traditional courthouse square during Ohio's period of greatest growth. Typically, the residence comprised the front portion of the building, usually an irregularly shaped two-story plan in the Queen Anne or High Victorian style, with the jail forming the rear of the building. The jail complemented the overall stylistic "design," with stone construction and architectural details conveying the stronghold nature of the lock-up. The combination sheriff's residence and jail buildings were prominently located either next to the courthouse or close by on an adjacent block facing the courthouse square.

1880–1930: THE GOLDEN AGE OF OHIO COURTHOUSES

From the decades following the end of the Civil War through the early twentieth century, Ohio was one of the most powerful and diverse economic and industrial centers in the United States. Overall, Ohio reflected the growth seen by the country as a whole during this period. Ohio's population was a cross section of America, ranking among the top states in population and with that a large electoral delegation making the state a political force. By the end of the 1920s, Ohio was the fourth most populous state. This period ushered in the golden age of Ohio courthouses with the construction of nearly fifty new buildings.

Architecturally, the courthouses of this period reflect the national impact of Henry Hobson Richardson and the return to classical traditions of the Renaissance Revival and Beaux-Arts eclecticism. Richardson's work was extensively published in architectural journals and publications during the 1880s, making it highly influential. Edward O. Fallis's design for the 1888–91 Williams County Courthouse in Bryan in northwest Ohio, is Richardsonian in its overall balance and symmetry, contrasting red brick and rock-faced stone trim and details, and steeply pitched roof with tile-crowned

Photo: Christopher Riley

Fig. 6. Miami County Courthouse, Troy, by Joseph Warren Yost, 1885–88.

Photo: Nyttend via Wikimedia Commons

Fig. 7. Putnam County Courthouse, Ottawa, by Frank L. Packard, 1912–13.

turrets. The 1895–97 Trumbull County Courthouse in Warren by Labelle & French shows the large arches, deep window reveals and door openings, overall masonry, rock-faced stone piers with foliated capitals, and round towers and turrets characteristic of Richardson's designs, while the 1894–96 design of the Wood County Courthouse in Bowling Green by Yost & Packard resembles Richardson's Allegheny County Courthouse in Pennsylvania.

The courthouse designs of Columbus-based Joseph Warren Yost and Frank L. Packard demonstrate the architects' expertise in classical revivals, drawing from the historical precedents of ancient Greece, Rome, and the Italian Renaissance in Yost's Beaux-Arts–style Miami County Courthouse (Troy, 1885–88; fig. 6) and Packard's Renaissance Revival design for the Putnam County Courthouse (Ottawa, 1912–13; fig. 7). Likewise, Cleveland architect J. Milton Dyer shows his Beaux-Arts training in his Renaissance Revival style for the Stark County Courthouse in Canton, completed in 1894, and a richly detailed Beaux-Arts opulence in the 1907 Lake County Courthouse in Painesville built adjacent to the earlier temple-front courthouse that was converted to the City Hall.

These magnificent courthouses reflect the national City Beautiful movement dedicated to a public architecture of beauty, dignity, and utility. The City Beautiful movement created a new sense of civic grandeur, seen in the unified classical courthouse exteriors, interiors adorned with murals and sculpture, and patriotic statues on the courthouse square celebrating Ohio's military contributions.

1930–70: MODERN BLENDS OF COURTHOUSE CLASSICISM

The final period of historic courthouse design in Ohio shows the impact of the Great Depression and New Deal programs followed by postwar growth and renewed prosperity. The courthouses designed during the 1930s–60s abandoned the earlier forms for stripped classicism and the modernist, but still classically inspired structures of New Formalism.

The courthouse for the last of Ohio's eighty-eight counties to organize, Noble, in southeast Ohio, was built in 1933–34 and occupied the central courthouse square in the town of Caldwell. Designed by architect Charles J. Marr and funded by the federal Works Progress Administration (WPA), the three-story brick building, containing murals depicting local history, has a stone arcaded entrance and upper floors articulated by stylized stone Ionic pilasters spaced between multipaned windows with stripped-down classically detailed pediments, stone beltcourses, and a stone parapet. Vinton County's 1933–39 courthouse in McArthur is another New Deal construction. The stripped classical yellow brick building with stylized classical architectural details was a WPA-funded project that, like the Noble courthouse, used local bricks. The 1940s–50s saw new courthouses constructed after fires destroyed the buildings in Jackson, Champaign, and Portage counties.

In the 1960s, the controversial replacement of Richland County's nineteenth-century brick courthouse in Mansfield, which suffered the impact of deferred maintenance and the mid-century disdain for Victorian era architecture, was an example of classical principles interpreted in modern materials by local architect Thomas G. Zaugg & Associates. The building's most distinctive feature is the three-story cast-concrete colonnade running along its front. The new courthouse faced the site of the earlier structure, which became a landscaped plaza, with the new complex located adjacent to the historic town square, also altered by a postwar street running through its center. While new courthouse construction was still the exception rather than the norm, the 1980s saw new courthouse complexes built in Warren (with historic courthouse retained), Gallia (due to courthouse fire), and Franklin Counties.

BEYOND THE TWENTIETH CENTURY: RENEWING THE PAST

By the twenty-first century, threats to Ohio's historic courthouses were increasing as a result of deferred maintenance, the need for larger facilities, the demands of new technology, and often-inaccurate perceptions that renovation would cost more than new construction. In 2012, the pressures facing historic courthouses culminated in the highly publicized, politically heated demolition of the Elijah Myers–designed Beaux-Arts Seneca County Courthouse (Tiffin, 1884–86), to be replaced in 2017 by the Seneca County Justice Center, a faux Second Empire–style building connected to a replica of a nineteenth-century commercial building. Aside from this faint homage to nineteenth-century courthouse architecture, the demolition raised much awareness of the value of investing in the preservation of Ohio's courthouses from the 1800s. This has spurred initiatives such as Licking County's ten-year project to renovate its courthouse exterior, ornate courtroom, and interior artwork, celebrated with a rededication in May 2025, and the Van Wert County Courthouse renovation of the building's Common Pleas Courtroom and majestic dome. These two examples, along with others, demonstrate that the county courthouse, a symbol of justice and local pride, by continuing to serve modern-day governmental needs, can have a renewed life as the "finest building of its kind."[10]

Barbara Powers is emerita State Historic Preservation Office, Ohio History Connection, with forty-two years of experience in historic survey and National Register of Historic Places programs. She served as the state coordinator for the Society of Architectural Historians' online publication *Archipedia, Ohio's 100 Classic Buildings*, 2013–19. Her published works include "Ohio's Pride, the Art and Architecture of the Ohio State Office Building" (*Timeline*, 2006); "Louis Bromfield's Big House at Malabar Farm: Form Follows Fiction" in *Re-creating the American Past, Essays on the Colonial Revival* (University of Virginia Press, 2006), and "The Architecture of the Ohio Governor's Residence" in *Our First Family's Home* (Ohio University Press, 2008). She holds a master's degree in architectural history from the University of Virginia.

Notes

Epigraph: Helen Hooven Santmyer, *Ohio Town: A Portrait of Xenia, Ohio* (New York: HarperCollins, 1984; originally published 1962), 21.

1. Susan W. Thrane, *County Courthouses of Ohio* (Bloomington: Indiana University Press, 2000), 13.

2. Additionally, Ohio's early statehouses in Chillicothe (1803), Zanesville (1810), and Columbus (1812) were built in the foursquare form.

3. Marion M. Ohman, "Diffusion of Foursquare Courthouses to the Midwest 1785–1885," *Geographical Review* 72, no. 2 (April 1982): 171–89.

4. E. S. Colborn and A. A. Graham, eds., *History of Fairfield and Perry Counties, Ohio* (Chicago: W.H. Beers & Co., 1883), 55.

5. Neville H. Clouten, "The Old Montgomery County Court House, Dayton, Ohio," *Journal of the Society of Architectural Historians* 26, no. 4 (December 1967): 296. The public enters the building from the front portico and proceeds up the spiral stairs to the gallery overlooking the courtroom. The sheriff and recorder enter on the left side of the courtroom from their offices on the first floor. The judge's chamber is on the second "floor," reaching the courtroom from a private enclosed stair. The jury comes in from the right side of the courtroom, and the prisoner enters from the jail at the rear of the courthouse.

6. Clouten, "Old Montgomery County Court House," 300.

7. Ibid.

8. Thrane, *County Courthouses of Ohio*, 14. The county courthouse administrative offices included three county commissioners, a county engineer, recorder, auditor, treasurer, prosecuting attorney, sheriff, board of elections, coroner, public defender, and boards and commissions illustrating the growing complexity of government functions and responsibilities at the county level. In 1912, the Ohio Constitution was amended to eliminate the judicial districts and subdivisions, replaced by the election of Common Pleas Court judges in each county.

9. Thrane, *County Courthouses of Ohio*, 11.

10. Paraphrased from newspaper articles covering the dedication of new courthouses, such as the Hancock County Courthouse in *The Times-Democrat* (Lima), August 13, 1884, 3: "a magnificent and imposing structure, large enough and grand enough for the capital of the state"; and the Miami County Courthouse in the *Urbana Daily Citizen*, January 31, 1888, 2: "building one of the finest in the state."

SAVING THE OHIO STATEHOUSE

FROM DESIGN TO RESTORATION

ROBERT D. LOVERSIDGE

Constructed between 1839 and 1861, and in continuous use since then, the Ohio Statehouse has been widely celebrated as a symbol of state prominence and architectural achievement. At the time of its completion, it was second in size only to the U.S. Capitol, and nearly as admired. Thomas O'Donnell, in a 1925 article in *Architectural Forum*, stated that "one of the finest examples of Greek Revival in America is the capitol at Columbus, Ohio."[1] Even Frank Lloyd Wright, who was not known for his praise of historic buildings, called the Ohio Statehouse the "most honest of all American Statehouses."[2]

Since its inception, the Statehouse has witnessed nearly every important event in Ohio history. Abraham Lincoln campaigned here; as president-elect he spoke to the state's General Assembly about the possibility of civil war; and he lay in state in the building's rotunda after his assassination, where he was visited by over 50,000 people within just a few hours.

Remarkable for its conical roof and cupola, the Ohio Statehouse is the result of the work of a succession of notable architects and designers. This work culminated at the end of the twentieth century in a comprehensive restoration, renovation, and addition project that prepared the building for its ongoing service as a state capitol and iconic architectural presence into the twenty-first century.

DESIGN COMPETITION, 1838

By the 1830s, the original (1816) Columbus statehouse and an adjacent state office building had proved to be too small, and a competition was held to develop a design for a new capitol building.[3] The building's design, which spanned twenty-two years and included multiple architects, started as the result of a national competition in 1838. The competition circular said this about the proposed style: "The Grecian Doric order is suggested; but not with a view of governing exclusively in the choice."[4] This strictly American interpretation of classical Greek design was favored in the new nation as a departure from the popular European styles of the day. "For public architecture, Greek temples had two particularly desirable qualities—they were splendid to look upon, and they could be built to suit nearly any budget."[5]

The competition attracted some sixty entries, from which the Statehouse Commissioners, appointed to oversee the new building, awarded three prizes: the first prize went to Cincinnati architect Henry Walter, the second to New York City architect Martin E. Thompson, and the third to Hudson Valley landscape painter Thomas Cole. The commissioners informed the state legislature that any of the awarded designs would be satisfactory. The legislators then left the decision (or indecision) up to the commissioners. They traveled to eastern U.S. cities to look at buildings and talk to architects, ultimately hiring the well-known New York architect Alexander Jackson Davis to evaluate the winning entries and develop a "composite" design taking hints from the three competition winners. He also added his own touches.

Davis's composite design established the simple rectangular form with four prominent facades, a continuous Doric entablature, and recessed loggias with Doric columns in antis. The design also called for a rotunda capped with a rather large dome. Although the Greeks did not routinely employ domes in their buildings, the concept of a central,

Fig. 1. Ohio Statehouse, Columbus, by William Russell West, Nathan B. Kelley, Isaiah Rogers, and others, 1839–61.

Photo: © Brad Feinknopf

daylit space became a common feature of American state capitol buildings. Davis's design, however, was rejected as being too expensive.

DESIGN AND CONSTRUCTION, 1839–61

Competition winner Henry Walter was named architect, and construction commenced in early 1839 without a final design, using convict labor from the nearby penitentiary. It was agreed that any subsequent design refinements could be accommodated within the foundations that Walter began. The cornerstone was placed, with appropriate ceremony, on July 4, 1839, and some limited work began on-site. Later in the year, the Ohio General Assembly repealed the legislation authorizing the construction and began reconsidering whether Columbus should remain Ohio's capital city. While this debate went on for the next several years, the foundations were covered over, and residents were allowed to graze cows on the square.

Meanwhile, to provide material for the foundation, the state purchased a nearby limestone quarry for $15,000. Finally, in 1846, a new Statehouse Act was passed, keeping Columbus as the capital city, and construction restarted until funds again ran out in 1847. In February of 1848, Philadelphia architect William Russell West was appointed to supervise the project. West proposed a number of changes to the design, including elimination of some windows and the addition of a slightly recessed pedimented attic above the west and east loggias. He also proposed a cupola featuring a conical roof, in place of the domes suggested by the competition winners and by Davis.

Work was slowed in 1850 due to a cholera outbreak that claimed nearly 200 workers. In 1851, a short railroad was built to connect the stone quarry directly to the downtown construction site. In 1852, a new Statehouse Act was passed, with new commissioners and a desire for a more efficient project. West was retained as architect, although he endured some criticism. Also in 1852, the old 1816 State House, built into a corner of the ten-acre Capitol Square, burned, adding pressure to complete the new building.

In 1854, West resigned under duress and, in a dispute over his authority, was replaced by prominent Columbus architect Nathan B. Kelley. Kelley began by measuring the work in place, as West had taken all his drawings with him when he left. The absence of interior plans and the nearly unfinished nature of the space gave Kelley the opportunity to leave his mark on the building. By this time, architectural tastes were moving away from the austere Greek Revival to a more florid and ornamented

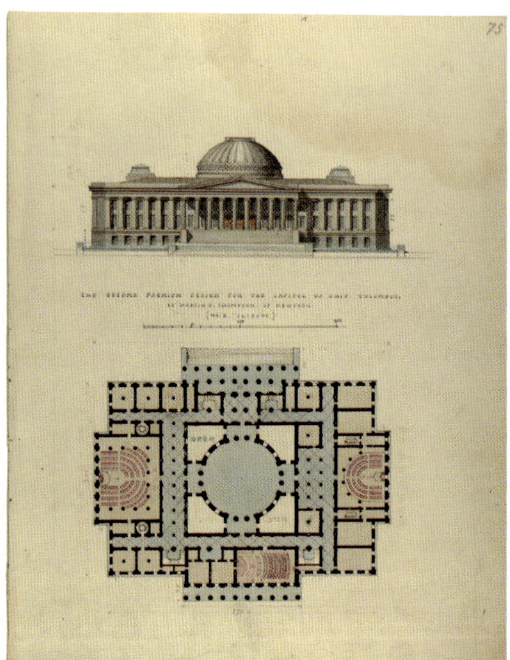

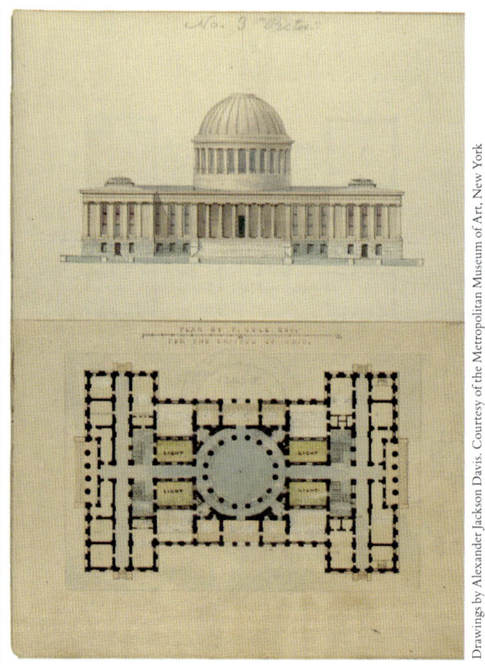

Drawings by Alexander Jackson Davis. Courtesy of the Metropolitan Museum of Art, New York

Fig. 2. Winners of the 1838 competition for the design of the Ohio Statehouse: first prize, Henry Walter; second prize, Martin E. Thompson; third prize, Thomas Cole.

Photo: Courtesy of the Kelton House Museum and Garden via Ohio Memory

Fig. 3. Funeral procession of President Abraham Lincoln passing the completed Ohio Statehouse. Lithograph, c. 1865.

style, and Kelley's interiors started to follow this trend. Kelley also added a central heating and ventilating system to the design, and his final floor plans are close to what was built. In addition, he returned to the earlier design of a dome over the rotunda.

In 1856, concerns about design changes and rapidly escalating costs led to another Statehouse Act and new commissioners, who consulted with nationally distinguished architects Thomas U. Walter and Richard Upjohn for opinions. Their report criticized the interiors as being too elaborate, among other issues. West and Kelley naturally objected, and very few changes were actually made. However, Walter and Upjohn also recommended reverting back to a conical roof in place of the dome.

Although there was still much work to be done, by 1857 the legislative halls were complete enough for use, and a grand 24-hour-long celebration was held, attended by, "with a close approximation of accuracy, 10,728" people.[6]

In 1858, Isaiah Rogers, a renowned architect then located in Cincinnati, was appointed to "finish" the building. Rogers wanted to make a number of dramatic changes that were not enacted, including enlarging the cupola by surrounding it with a colonnade of cast-iron columns, and adding a projecting portico on the west front. By 1861, the Statehouse was considered complete, although final paint schemes and other decorating was not done until just after the Civil War.

THE COMPLETED STATEHOUSE, 1861

Notably, all the designs contained a round central rotunda capped on the outside by either a shallow dome (like the original wooden dome of the U.S. Capitol) or a conical roof. This predated the post–Civil War fashion of having a large dome on newer capitol buildings.[7] The completed Statehouse features a conical roof over a two-story cupola containing an observation promenade and a large skylight to provide natural illumination to the rotunda.[8]

While the Statehouse is not modeled after any particular building from antiquity, the exterior contains elements typical of Greek buildings like the Parthenon. The design of the cupola may have been influenced by the ancient Greek temple form known as tholos. As a practical product of its time, the building has windows for natural light, and, by the time it was completed, gas lights and a central heating system. The structure, however, demonstrates the way buildings were constructed for a thousand years—

Photo: Joseph Sohm/Shutterstock

Fig. 4. Western facade of the restored Ohio Statehouse.

with thick brick and stone bearing walls, brick vaults, stone floors, and no steel or reinforced concrete.

Finally, after twenty-two arduous years of design, politics, economics, and construction, it could be said that "the Ohio state capitol takes rank with the work of Mills or of Strickland, or with [Isaiah] Rogers's own Merchants' Exchange in New York, as representing the very best ideals of the Greek Revival movement expressed in public buildings. Its great scale, its superb and daring simplicity, and its originality all make it one of the most distinguished monuments of native American architecture."[9]

EXPANSION AND THE JUDICIARY ANNEX, 1901–33

When the Statehouse opened in 1857, it housed virtually all of state government. After the Civil War, as Ohio asserted itself as a politically and economically powerful state, government naturally expanded. Changes became necessary, beginning with subdividing some of the larger rooms, and continuing with filling in some of the open courts that provided light and air to the internal areas of the building. In the 1880s, some of the public spaces were redecorated in the then-popular Victorian style.

Several proposals to enlarge the building followed. These included adding wings, a floor, or a high-rise tower. Any one of these would have greatly altered the elegant Grecian building. In the end, a more refined solution was developed. In 1901, an annex building, designed in the Neoclassical Revival style by the Cincinnati architectural firm Samuel Hannaford and Sons, was constructed adjacent to the Statehouse building. Named the Judiciary Annex, it housed the state's Supreme Court and a number of other offices, freeing up space in the capitol for expansion. The Annex is a "modern" steel-framed building with electric lights, but its classical style and matching limestone exterior make it an architecturally compatible addition to the 1861 Statehouse.

As government continued to expand, several additional state office buildings were constructed in Columbus, including the 1933 Ohio State Office Building in the Art Moderne style designed by Harry Hake of Cincinnati, located a block away in the "new" riverfront civic district.[10]

RESTORATION AND ADDITION, 1988–96

In the second half of the twentieth century, two state government buildings were added near the Statehouse. In 1974, the forty-story James A. Rhodes State Office Tower, designed by Brubaker/Brandt of Columbus and Dalton, Dalton, Little, and Newport of Cleveland, was constructed across the street from Capitol Square. A little over a decade later, another skyscraper was being contemplated. Acknowledging the overcrowding—if not the deteriorated condition—of the Statehouse, the Ohio House of Representatives decided to move all ninety-nine of their member offices to the new building, the thirty-two-story Vern Riffe Center for Government and the Arts, designed by NBBJ of Columbus and opened in 1988 across the street from the Statehouse. Their hearing rooms, clerks, and legislative chambers—all their public functions—would remain in the historic capitol, which had been designated a National Historic Landmark by the U.S. Department of the Interior in 1978.

At the same time, the Ohio Senate decided that it would not move to the new building but would renovate the dilapidated and mostly vacant Judiciary Annex as offices for its thirty-three members. Over the years, as both buildings—connected by a concrete terrace over a leaky garage—deteriorated, they had become coupled in many ways.[11] They shared the same antiquated heating system, with steam being delivered from underground pipes originating at the old state penitentiary several blocks away. State Architect Carole Olshavsky convinced the legislative leadership to commission a master plan for the entire site that could guide redevelopment of the Statehouse once the Riffe Center was completed.

Photo: Ryan McGinnis/Alamy Stock Photo

Fig. 5. Under the Rotunda of the restored Ohio Statehouse.

By 1988, more than a century of neglect and careless alteration had created a dire need for renewal. The main structure—originally containing 53 rooms, each with access to natural light—had been subdivided into 317 rooms. Intermediate floors were added in tall spaces, and rooms were remodeled with several generations of dropped ceilings that obscured vaults, skylights, and decorative details. Practically every electrical and mechanical system developed since the mid-nineteenth century had been added, including ninety-three separate air-conditioning systems.

Columbus-based Schooley Caldwell Associates was selected, along with a team of experts, to evaluate space needs and the condition of the buildings, to design a long-range plan for restoration, and subsequently to carry out the project.[12] Senator Richard Finan was appointed to lead the project for the state.[13]

There were no "as-built" drawings of existing conditions, so, as had been the case for architect Nathan B. Kelley in the nineteenth century, the first task was to hand-measure (no laser scanning was available yet) the entire building. Extensive research was also conducted into the surviving building fabric, the architectural history of the structures, and the changing processes of government.

Phased construction began in earnest in 1989 and was substantially complete in July 1996. The design challenge of this project was to extend and expand the useful life of the Statehouse for another century, by solving programmatic issues to ensure active continuing use of the building as the state capitol, and to restore the essential characteristics of the Greek Revival building.

More than 250 infill rooms were removed and replaced by rooms with vaulted ceilings, skylights, and reproduction gas light fixtures. Interior spaces included restored or replicated original woodwork, marble, mosaic tile, carpets, fireplace surrounds, decorative plaster, stained glass, sculpture, and historic paint colors. The public spaces, including the legislative halls and the governor's office, were painstakingly restored. Original light courts were reopened to house necessary egress stairs and glass-enclosed elevators. Natural light was reintroduced everywhere. Work on the cupola included a new skylight and a restored laylight featuring a stained-glass seal of Ohio.

Photo: Schooley Caldwell

Fig. 6. Ohio Senate Building (Judiciary Annex) by Samuel Hannaford and Sons, 1901, and Capitol Atrium by Schooley Caldwell, 1993.

The nineteenth-century capitol lacked spaces to accommodate large gatherings and visitor services. To address this need, Schooley Caldwell designed an addition, with an architectural presence of its own, linking the Statehouse and the Senate Building (the old Judiciary Annex). Known as the Capitol Atrium, it is structurally attached to its historic neighbors only by a continuous skylight. A new quarry was opened to extract "Columbus Limestone" to match the original local stone used to construct the historic Statehouse. The Schooley Caldwell team determined that Samuel Hannaford must have anticipated such an addition when he designed the Annex, as the floor levels of the two buildings are aligned.

The first week of July 1996 was filled with a series of free public events celebrating the renewed pride of the state in its historic capitol. These included events for the hundreds of craftspeople and laborers; events for the downtown "neighbors" of the capitol, who had witnessed the long construction effort; and a July 4 public open house attended by 20,000 people.

A STATEHOUSE SERVING THE TWENTY-FIRST CENTURY

One of the most important accomplishments of the restoration was creation of the Capitol Square Review and Advisory Board (CSRAB), a bipartisan governing board with the dual charges of supporting good government operations at the Capitol and maintaining the historic integrity of the landmark. Significantly, while changes have been made, they are carefully monitored by CSRAB so that none violate the spirit of the restoration design.[14] In addition, the nonprofit Capitol Square Foundation raises millions of dollars to enhance the ongoing educational mission of the Statehouse.[15]

The eight-year, 280,000-square foot, $121-million[16] public project revitalized the Statehouse and the Judiciary Annex and created a distinguished addition. Public visitation to the Statehouse expanded fivefold in the first year after reopening, and it continues to grow. In 1838, the Statehouse commissioners, upon awarding prizes for the design competition, observed that "in its exterior form and interior disposition of apartments there should be united that beauty and grandeur which the rules of art require, and which comport with the dignity and wealth of the State. The degree of civilization and knowledge prevailing in a community is always clearly designated by its works of art, and by none more than by its architecture; it is then at least desirable that Ohio should not be behind that degree of improvement in the arts which the American people have attained."[17] Over the nearly 200 years that followed, the Ohio Statehouse has successfully survived threats of obsolescence, economic crises, and political turmoil, among other major events. Its significant rehabilitation at the end of the twentieth century set the stage for yet another century of "beauty and grandeur" and public use of Ohio's landmark capitol.

Robert D. Loversidge is an award-winning preservation design architect, a Fellow of the American Institute of Architects (AIA), and the recently retired CEO of Schooley Caldwell. He is a past chair of the AIA's National Historic Resources Committee and a recipient of the AIA Ohio Gold Medal. Loversidge is a graduate of The Ohio State University's Knowlton School of Architecture and a Distinguished Alumnus of the university's College of Engineering. While at Schooley Caldwell, he was principal-in-charge of the renovation of the Ohio Statehouse, where he still serves as an advisor, and of the Thomas J. Moyer Ohio Judicial Center, home to the Supreme Court of Ohio.

Notes

1. Thomas O'Donnell. "The Greek Revival Capitol at Columbus, Ohio," *Architectural Forum* 42, no. 1 (June 1925): 5

2. Frank Lloyd Wright, quoted in Chris Matheney, *Cornerstone to Cupola: The Ohio Statehouse*, (Wilmington, OH: Orange Frazer Press, 2017), 32.

3. The first Columbus statehouse was actually Ohio's third. Earlier ones had been built in Chillicothe and Zanesville, the state's previous capital cities.

4. Statehouse competition circular, dated April 10, 1838. Thomas Cole's copy is held by the New York State Library.

5. Henry-Russell Hitchcock and William Seale, *Temples of Democracy: The State Capitols of the U.S.A.* (New York: Harcourt Brace Jovanovich, 1979), 83.

6. Jacob Henry Studer, *Columbus, Ohio: Its History, Resources, and Progress* (Columbus, OH: W. Riches, Engraver, 1873), 343.

7. During the Civil War, construction on the Capitol's cast-iron dome was briefly stopped, but President Lincoln said, "If people see the Capitol going on, it is a sign we intend the Union shall go on," so it was resumed. (Senate Stories: https://www.senate.gov/about/historic-buildings-spaces/capitol/dome-national-symbol.htm). Many veterans, upon settling in newer states after the war, insisted on their permanent capitols having domes like the one in Washington, DC, seen as a symbol of national unity.

8. Over the years, the cupola has been ridiculed as a "cheese box" (I. T. Frary, *Early Homes of Ohio* [Dover Publications, 1970; originally published in 1936 by Garrett & Massie], 211) and other less than complimentary terms. In the twenty-first century, a local newspaper featured this unique attribute in a front-page story entitled "Dome Envy?" (Eric Johns, "Dome Envy." *The Other Paper* [Columbus, OH], July 3, 2008, 1). During the restoration project that prepared the Ohio Statehouse for continuing service into the twenty-first century, the speaker of the Ohio House of Representatives instructed me, in my role as principal architect for the renovation, "Son, make sure we have enough money in the budget to put a dome on the Statehouse." I had to explain why we have no dome, why that makes our capitol unique, and, most importantly, why we should not add one. Luckily, he agreed.

9. Talbot Hamlin, *Greek Revival Architecture in America: Being an Account of Important Trends in American Architecture and American Life prior to the War Between the States* (New York, Dover Publications, 1964; originally published in 1944 by Oxford University Press), 289.

10. In 2004, this building was adapted into a permanent home for the Supreme Court of Ohio. It is now called the Thomas J. Moyer Ohio Judicial Center, after the late Ohio chief justice.

11. The terrace, which was a leftover from the original construction, was referred to as "Pigeon Run" by the legislative pages who had to duck birds as they scurried from Statehouse to Annex.

12. Schooley Caldwell Associates (architects and engineers), Moody Nolan (associate architects), Kabil Associates (structural engineers), Behnke & Associates and Schooley Caldwell Associates (landscape architects), Benjamin D. Rickey & Co. (historic preservation consultants), William Seale (historian), Ronald Keller (government relations), Fisher Marantz and Gary Steffy (lighting), Jaffe Holden (acoustics), Frank Matero (stone restoration), Chambers, Murphy & Burge (materials conservation), Darla Olson (decorative painting), McKay Lodge (fine arts conservation), and Preview Group (codes consultant). Sherman R. Smoot Company was the construction manager.

13. Senate President Stanley Aronoff, who appointed Finan, often said that he selected him "because he is stubborn, he represents a 'safe' district, and he loves the Statehouse."

14. A partial list of modifications and additions since the renovation includes the Ohio Veterans Plaza, George Washington Williams Room, Ladies' Gallery, Statehouse Museum, Museum Shop, Chase Education Center, bronze state seal and motto on the West Plaza, public bus shelters, and Ohio Holocaust Survivors and Liberators Memorial (designed by Daniel Libeskind).

15. Activities include restoration of significant artwork, design of interactive exhibits, recognition of significant contributions by Ohioans, a travel grant program to help bring thousands of students to the capitol, creation of an online civics curriculum, and display of the original Ohio Constitution in the Statehouse Museum.

16. $310 million in current dollars.

17. Studer, *Columbus, Ohio*, 334.

OHIO'S PRESIDENTIAL MEMORIALS

KAY FANNING

Between 1890 and 1927, five ambitious architectural memorials honoring four presidents native to Ohio—James A. Garfield, Ulysses S. Grant, William McKinley, and Warren G. Harding—were completed, with a more modest tribute erected to a fifth, Rutherford. B. Hayes. All of these memorials are situated in northern Ohio, apart from the Grant Memorial, which was built in New York City. They form a concentration of American commemorative architecture second only to the memorials defining the National Mall in Washington, D.C. This remarkable group reflects the important part Ohio played in the latter half of the nineteenth century and beginning of the twentieth as a hub of American industry, trade, and innovation. During the period following the Civil War, Ohio also assumed a central role in the formation and growth of the Republican Party. The state's thriving social and political economy supported the careers of seven Ohio-born U.S. presidents—the most of any state.[1]

Garfield, Grant, and McKinley were all Civil War veterans, and Grant was the Union's outstanding military hero; they were all also staunch Republicans. Their deaths, particularly the public assassinations of Garfield and McKinley, recalled the assassination of Abraham Lincoln, whose murder the day before Palm Sunday, in 1865, unleashed a flood of mourning across the North.[2] Garifield and McKinley's elaborate funeral ceremonies were modeled on those of Lincoln: their bodies lay in state in the U.S. Capitol Rotunda and black-draped trains carried their caskets back to hometowns or burial places, where memorial tombs were built and then dedicated in ceremonies presided over by sitting and former presidents.

Fig. 1. James A. Garfield Memorial, Cleveland, by George Keller, dedicated 1890.

The architects of Ohio's presidential memorials adapted classical prototypes for a modern secular democracy. They also made free use of varied Christian symbols, reflecting the broad cultural associations of Christian devotion in the late nineteenth and early twentieth centuries suggesting the righteousness of the Union cause and the attempt to find meaning in the assassinations of Lincoln, Garfield, and McKinley.

Several characteristics define these memorials. They are generally elevated to literally lift the deceased leader toward the heavens and ensure the memorials' visibility from a distance, with the visitor proceeding to them through a designed landscape. Constructed of fine stone masonry, they each enclose a primary space that is typically roofed by a dome and dominated by a statue of the president or by his tomb. Finally, each memorial is ornamented with artwork and inscriptions expressing the president's character and legacy.

JAMES A. GARFIELD MEMORIAL, 1890

Before the Garfield Memorial, only two presidential monuments had been built in the United States, both designed by architect Robert Mills to honor the first American president: the Washington Monument in Baltimore, Maryland, a 165-foot-tall marble column (1842); and the Washington Monument in Washington, DC, a 555-foot-tall marble obelisk (1848–84).[3] The use of vertical shafts was typical for the period.

In 1881, sixteen years after Lincoln's death, the twentieth American president, James A. Garfield (1831–1881), was assassinated shortly after taking office. He was entombed within a memorial that demonstrated new architectural ambitions, signifying the post–Civil War consolidation and growth of the United States and the rising status of Ohio (fig. 1).[4]

Raised in poverty outside Cleveland—the last president to be born in a log cabin—Garfield overcame the difficulties of his childhood to become a lay preacher, a college president, an Ohio state senator, and an eight-term congressman in the U.S. House of Representatives. In 1880, as a dark-horse candidate, Garfield was elected to the presidency. His brief term in office was mostly spent dealing with people asking for federal employment.

In July 1881, Garfield was shot twice by a deranged office seeker; one bullet lodged in his back. At his request, the invalid Garfield was moved to coastal New Jersey, where he died on September 19. A funeral train carried his body to Washington and then to Cleveland, where the casket lay on public view within a huge black-draped pavilion before being moved to a receiving vault in picturesque Lake View Cemetery.[5] Influential friends—including former president Rutherford B. Hayes, statesman and, later, secretary of state John Hay, and oil magnate John D. Rockefeller, the richest man in the country—formed the Garfield National Memorial Association to sponsor a design competition for a commemorative tomb, won by architect George Keller in 1883.[6]

Photo: iStock.com/zrfphoto

Fig. 2. Interior of the Garfield Memorial.

The tomb's wealth of Romantic associations celebrated Garfield not only as president but as a symbol of Ohio. Keller took inspiration from numerous precedents: imperial Roman tombs, early Christian and medieval chapels—particularly the fifth-century St. Vitale, in Ravenna, Italy, and the eighth-century Palatine Chapel at Charlemagne's Palace at Aachen (Aix-la-Chapelle), Germany—and eighteenth-century garden follies.

The Garfield National Memorial Association proclaimed Keller's design to be the first real mausoleum built to honor an American statesman.[7] As a building shaped by its interior space, it was a striking change from the columns and obelisks of earlier American memorials. The tomb is composed of a cylindrical tower, 180 feet high and constructed of heavily rusticated blocks of Ohio sandstone, bearing a conical roof that encloses an interior dome. A complex artistic program unites Christian iconography with national and state symbols, expressed through sculpture, painting, and glass and stone mosaics.[8] A ring of stained-glass windows depicts allegorical female figures representing the thirteen original colonies plus Ohio. On the gold mosaic surface of the saucer dome, evergreen wreaths, representing each American state and territory, and four winged figures symbolize "earthly glory and heavenly immortality"[9] (fig. 2).

At its dedication on Memorial Day 1890, thousands gathered at the memorial to hear an impressive roster of speakers, including President Benjamin Harrison, former president Rutherford B. Hayes, and future president William McKinley, along with aging Union heroes. Former governor Jacob D. Cox eulogized Garfield as an "apotheosis of Western Reserve manhood."[10]

The only High Victorian presidential memorial, the Garfield Memorial carries a potent mix of cultural ideas: veneration of Lincoln; Christian mourning for the loss of the Civil War generation; the rise of the Radical Republicans, with their support for both Black citizens and the business interests of the Gilded Age; and America's new ambitions to surpass its Western European cultural patrimony. Drawing on a wide array of sources, the memorial exemplifies an aesthetic that was soon to be abandoned for a new classical rigor.

GENERAL GRANT NATIONAL MEMORIAL, 1891

A new level of scholarly sophistication for national monuments was introduced with a memorial dedicated to an Ohio president but built in New York City. Ulysses S. Grant (1822–85) was born in southwest Ohio, where he lived until he entered the United States Military Academy at West Point, New York. The greatest general of the Union Army, Grant's military stature vaulted him into the presidency for two terms beginning in 1868.[11]

In 1884, sixteen years after leaving office, Grant was stricken with cancer of the jaw; he died on July 23, 1885. A site for a memorial tomb was selected near his home in New York City, on a bluff high above the Hudson River. Architect John H. Duncan won a competition sponsored by the Grant Monument Association with a proposal for a granite tomb. His primary source was the renowned early-fourth-century BCE Mausoleum of Halicarnassus, built for King Mausolus (d. 356 BCE), ruler of Halicarnassus on Asia Minor's Aegean coast.

Fig. 3. General Grant National Memorial, New York, by John H. Duncan, dedicated 1891.

Photo: Russell Kord ARCHIVE/Alamy Stock Photo

Towering on a bluff over New York City's harbor, Grant's stone mausoleum comprises a subterranean burial chamber surmounted by a high cubical base, supporting a temple crowned by a stepped pyramidal roof (fig. 3).[12] Duncan relied closely on an 1877 reconstruction of the Mausoleum of Halicarnassus by Stanislas-Louis Bernier.[13] Situated at the end of a long allee of trees, the Grant Memorial is composed of a Doric portico and a cubical cella supporting a cylindrical colonnaded drum, crowned with a conical roof over an interior dome.[14] Contrasting with the severe exterior, the interior of gray-veined white marble presents a softer, more sculptural appearance. At the center is an open, sunken crypt with the sarcophagi of Grant and his wife, Julia, inspired by Louis Visconti's Tomb of Napoleon (1843–53), at the Dôme des Invalides, in Paris.[15]

Ground was broken for the Grant Memorial in 1891, and it was dedicated in 1897. Between these years, there occurred a watershed in American architecture, the 1893 World's Columbian Exposition in Chicago, marking the 400th anniversary of Columbus's landing in the New World. The fair established a new scholarly paradigm for American civic architecture and city planning—a paradigm based on skillful adaptations of classical prototypes for buildings to house and, more important, to represent the ideals of a modern democracy.

MCKINLEY NATIONAL MEMORIAL, 1907

In September 1901, the twenty-fifth president, William McKinley (1843–1901), was shot by an anarchist as he stood at the head of a receiving line at the Pan-American Exposition in Buffalo, New York. He died eight days later, six months into his second term.

McKinley had fought in the Civil War in the regiment led by future president Rutherford B. Hayes. After the war, McKinley established a law practice in Canton, Ohio. Backed by the wealthy Ohio industrialist Marcus Alonzo Hanna, he soon entered politics; he was twice elected governor of Ohio before serving seven terms in the U.S. Congress. McKinley ran for president in a campaign organized by Hanna, which was conducted primarily from the front porch of McKinley's house in Canton.[16]

McKinley was a pro-business Republican who initiated America's rise as a colonial power and expanded its sphere of influence throughout the Caribbean, the Pacific, and Asia. Notably, he dispatched the American military to fight Spain in the Spanish-American War of 1898 and in the Philippine-American War of 1899–1902, ending Spanish rule in the Western hemisphere.

After his death, McKinley's powerful allies quickly arranged to build a national memorial tomb in a new garden cemetery in Canton (fig. 4). A memorial commission embarked on an unprecedented nationwide fundraising effort and held a national competition for a design, won by Harold Van Buren

Fig. 4. McKinley National Memorial, Canton, by Harold Van Buren Magonigle, dedicated 1907.

Magonigle in 1904. For his model, Magonigle chose the fifth-century CE mausoleum of the Ostrogoth King Theodoric—a Roman leader and Christian convert—in Ravenna, Italy, composed of a cylindrical stone chamber crowned by a massive monolithic dome.[17]

Magonigle's design throughout is simple but concentrated and imbued with Christian symbolism. He set his memorial at the top of a steep terraced hill, which rose at the end of a long, narrow reflecting pool. (The pool was removed in 1951.) The plan combines a sword and cross: "the cross of the martyr, the sword of the President in time of war"; the side and rear stairs form the hilt of the sword and three arms of the cross, while the main stairway represents the longer arm and, with the addition of the pool, creates the blade of the sword.[18] The mausoleum stands at the juncture of sword and cross, symbolizing the union of military strength and Christian piety in the person of McKinley.

NATIONAL MCKINLEY BIRTHPLACE MEMORIAL AND RUTHERFORD B. HAYES PRESIDENTIAL LIBRARY & MUSEUMS, 1915–16

Two other Ohio memorials present early examples of what today has become the primary type of presidential commemoration. The National McKinley Birthplace Memorial, in Niles (1915), and the Rutherford B. Hayes Presidential Library, in Fremont (1916), both combine libraries and museums as "living" memorials, fulfilling a practical as well as commemorative purpose. The white marble McKinley Birthplace Memorial was built by McKim, Mead & White near the site of McKinley's boyhood home; the Doric colonnade encircling its exterior opens to a courtyard, flanked on one side by the library and on the other by a McKinley museum (fig. 5).[19] Honoring the nineteenth president, the Hayes library (the first presidential library), a small sandstone Doric temple adjacent to the president's estate and burial place, houses the president's library and collections of local artifacts (fig. 6).

Photo: Stan Rohrer/Alamy Stock Photo

Fig. 5. National McKinley Birthplace Memorial, Niles, by McKim, Mead & White, 1915.

WARREN G. HARDING MEMORIAL, 1927

The last Ohio president, Warren G. Harding (1865–1923), was also commemorated in his hometown with an imposing architectural memorial. Harding, the twenty-ninth president, was a popular newspaper editor from the small city of Marion who was elected to the state senate and then the U.S. Senate. His conservative administration became identified with scandals—most notoriously, the selling of oil leases from federal reserves at Teapot Dome, Wyoming, by his secretary of the interior.[20]

Harding died of a stroke in San Francisco while on a nationwide train tour meant to regain the trust of the American people during a time of emerging disclosures about criminal behavior in his administration. His body was returned to Washington to lie in state in the Capitol and then to Marion for burial.

A Harding Memorial Association soon raised almost a million dollars, but contributions quickly fell as details emerged about the scandals—not only Teapot Dome but also the illegal selling of liquor licenses and Harding's extramarital affair with a young woman who later gave birth to their daughter. Nonetheless, the association held an invited design competition in 1925. The judges apparently favored a design by John Russell Pope for a small domed rotunda, until it was pointed out that it resembled a teapot; the submission of architect Henry Hornbostel was chosen instead.[21]

The Harding Memorial is a small, cylindrical temple of white marble, composed of a nested series of forms that subtly suggests the president's fall from grace (fig. 7). Unfluted Doric columns surround a wall, which in turn surrounds a small Ionic colonnade. Within the roofless enclosure, behind an aluminum fence, lie the twin graves of the Harding and his wife, Florence. Although completed by 1927, the memorial was not dedicated until 1931, when President Herbert Hoover was prevailed upon to appear at a small ceremony.[22]

Photo: Kristina Smith/Hayes Presidential Library & Museums

Fig. 6. Rutherford B. Hayes Presidential Library, Fremont, spearheaded by Webb C. Hayes, 1916.

CLASSICAL PRESIDENTIAL MEMORIALS AND THE LATER TWENTIETH CENTURY

By the early 1930s, American architectural practice was undergoing another profound transformation, as Beaux-Arts classicism was succeeded by European modernism for most major civic works. The memorial to Thomas Jefferson in Washington, DC, completed in 1943, a posthumous work by John Russell Pope modeled on the Roman Pantheon and Jefferson's Rotunda at the University of Virginia, would be the last classical memorial built in the United States until the World War II Memorial, dedicated in 2004 on the Mall.

As classical monuments, the Ohio memorials embody ideas about the attributes valued in national leaders and inevitably about the qualities held to be most definitive of the American nation and most worthy of emulation by its citizens. Architecture is joined with art to express notions of heroism and sacrifice as fundamental to the executive office and necessary for the fulfillment of America's destiny as a new world leader. They honor Ohioans who came from ordinary backgrounds; who—with the exception of Harding—were formed by their experiences of a war that threatened to tear the country apart; and who helped lead the reunited nation into a new prosperity.

Kay Fanning, historian at the U.S. Commission of Fine Arts (CFA), is the co-author with Thomas E. Luebke of *American Shrines: The Architecture of Presidential Commemoration* (University of Massachusetts Press, 2025), and a contributing writer to the CFA publications *Palace of State: The Eisenhower Executive Office Building* (2018) and *Civic Art: A Centennial History of the U.S. Commission of Fine Arts* (2013). She previously worked for the National Park Service and received her PhD in architectural history from the University of Virginia.

Photo: Stan Rohrer/Alamy Stock Photo

Fig. 7. Warren G. Harding Memorial, Marion, by Henry Hornbostel, 1927.

Notes

1. William Henry Harrison (1773–1841), who was born in Virginia and spent much of his adult life in Ohio, is sometimes claimed as an eighth Ohio president. His grandson, Benjamin Harrison (1833–1901), who was born in Ohio but as an adult lived in Indiana, also served as president. Neither Harrison has an architectural tomb or other memorial in Ohio. Cincinnati-born President William Howard Taft (1857–1930) was buried in Arlington National Cemetery, his grave marked by an elegant classical stele of red granite by the renowned sculptor James Earle Fraser.

2. See Merrill D. Peterson, *Lincoln in American Memory* (New York: Oxford University Press, 1995).

3. See Pamela Scott, "Robert Mills and American Monuments," in *Robert Mills, Architect*, ed. John A. Bryan (Washington, DC: AIA Press, 1989), and Kirk Savage, *Monument Wars: Washington, DC, the National Mall, and the Transformation of the Memorial Landscape* (Berkeley, CA: University of California Press, 2009).

4. Allan Peskin, *Garfield* (Kent, OH: Kent State University Press, 1978, 1999), and David Dyer, "James A. Garfield," in *The American Presidency*, ed. Alan Brinkley and Davis Dyer (New York: Houghton Mifflin Harcourt, 2004) 224–32.

5. John Clarke Ridpath, *The Life and Work of James A. Garfield* (Cincinnati, OH: Jones Brothers, 1881).

6. Garfield Memorial Committee, *The Man and the Mausoleum: Dedication of the Garfield Memorial Structure in Cleveland, Ohio, May 30, 1890* (Cleveland, OH: The Cleveland Printing and Publishing Co., 1890, reprinted 1924).

7. Garfield Memorial Committee, *Man and the Mausoleum*, 18.

8. Garfield Memorial Committee, *Man and the Mausoleum*, 34.

9. Garfield Memorial Committee, *Man and the Mausoleum*, 32.

10. Garfield Memorial Committee, *Man and the Mausoleum*, 90.

11. See Ron Chernow, *Grant* (New York: Penguin Random House, 2018), and William S. McFeely, *Grant* (New York: Norton, 1982 [1981]).

12. Howard Colvin, *Architecture and the After-Life* (New Haven, CT: Yale University Press, 1991), chap. 3.

13. See Chernow, *Grant*, 951; McFeely, *Grant*, 509; "A Hero Finds Rest," *New York Times*, July 24, 1885, 1; and other accounts in the *New York Times*, July 24, 25, and 29, 1885, and August 5, 6, and 9, 1885.

14. David M. Kahn, "The Grant Monument," *Journal of the Society of Architectural Historians* 41 (October 1982): 212–13, 228–29.

15. Kahn, "Grant Monument," 226–30.

16. Robert W. Merry, *President McKinley: Architect of the American Century* (New York: Simon & Schuster, 2018), 425–30.

17. The papers of the McKinley National Memorial Association are in the collections of the McKinley Museum at the Stark County Historical Society in Canton, OH. The most valuable material includes the book of press clippings, called *McKinley Tomb*, and six files: McKinley National Memorial, 1907–1917; McKinley National Memorial Dedication; McKinley, Wm., McKinley National Memorial Association; McKinley, Wm., McKinley National Memorial, Canton, Ohio; McKinley Monument—Construction, Letters, Bills Telegrams, Statements; and Memorials—Models. Also important are the dedication booklet, *The McKinley National Memorial* (Canton, 1907), and *Nation's Memorial to William McKinley, Canton* (c. 1913).

The single most valuable source of information on the McKinley Memorial is an essay by Magonigle, "A Description of the McKinley Memorial at Canton, Ohio, by the Architect," in Frederic S. Hartzell, *The National McKinley Memorial Association, Canton, Ohio, Together with Authentic Historical Data Relating to McKinley's Life and Public Services* (1913), 35–53, in the Stark County Historical Society file "McKinley, Wm. McKinley National Memorial, Canton, Ohio."

18. Hartzell, *National McKinley Memorial Association*, 36.

19. Webb Hayes (1856–1934) was a founder of the National Carbon Company, which later became Union Carbide. On Hayes's establishment of the library, see Thomas A. Smith, "Creation of the Nation's First Presidential Library and Museum: A Study in Cooperation," *Hayes Historical Journal*, Rutherford B. Hayes Presidential Library and Museum website, www.rbhayes.org/research/hayes-historical-journal-creation-of-the-nations-first-presidential-library-and-museum, accessed July 25, 2024. Many thanks to Barbara Powers of the Ohio History Connection for providing this information on the Hayes Library. Barbara Powers, State Historic Preservation Office, Ohio History Connection, "Re: Architects of the Rutherford B. Hayes Library," email, June 28, 2024.

20. Information on Harding comes from Paula S. Fass, "Warren G. Harding," in *The American Presidency*, ed. Alan Brinkley and Davis Dyer (New York: Houghton Mifflin Harcourt, 2004), 314–22; Francis Russell, *The Shadow of Blooming Grove: Warren G. Harding in His Times* (New York: McGrawHill, 1968); and Eugene P. Trani and David L. Wilson, *The Presidency of Warren G. Harding* (Lawrence, KS: University Press of Kansas, 1977). See also the dedication program, "Dedication of the Warren G. Harding Memorial" (1931); Ohio Historical Society, "Warren Gamaliel Harding" (n.d.); and C. B. Galbreath, "Warren Gamaliel Harding," *Ohio Archaeological and Historical Society Publications* 32 (1923): 555–70.

21. This story is from Russell, *Shadow of Blooming Grove* (p. 624), although the endnotes do not say where the author obtained the account.

22. Russell, *Shadow of Blooming Grove*, 624, 640; Robert S. Harper, "Harding's Haunted Tomb," *Plain Talk* 7 (September–October 1930): 349–56. Harper, an editor of the *Ohio State Journal*, also noted the memorial's resemblance to European ruins, comparing it to the tombs lining the Appian Way outside Rome.

CLEVELAND'S URBAN LANDSCAPES

TRANSFORMING THE INDUSTRIAL CITY

STEPHANIE RYBERG-WEBSTER & THOMAS W. HILDE

Situated where the Cuyahoga River meets Lake Erie, Cleveland rose to prominence as an industrial powerhouse in the late 1800s and early 1900s, producing steel and serving as shipping hub on the Ohio and Erie Canal system. By 1920, it was the nation's fifth-largest city. Industrial cities conjure images of smoke-belching factories, crowded working-class neighborhoods, and heavy infrastructure like railroads and bridges. Yet, industrialization also brought immense wealth to Cleveland. To counter the grime, disorder, and overcrowding that accompanied industry, wealthy local leaders in the early twentieth century turned to architecture and urban design to transform portions of the city's landscape, drawing on the order and elegance of the City Beautiful movement and classically inspired architecture. The resulting monumental urban landscapes—the downtown civic center of the Group Plan, and the arts and cultural center of the University Circle district, knitted together via the historic Public Square and the prominent Euclid Avenue—form a network of grand spaces and landmark buildings that reflect the city's stature and prosperity during the industrial era.

By the second half of the twentieth century, deindustrialization and population decline had changed Cleveland's fortunes dramatically, bringing deterioration and abandonment. Amid this post-industrial landscape, however, the legacy of Cleveland's industrial wealth persisted. In the twenty-first century, the imprint of the city's early monumental landscapes offers a cohesive framework for reimagining Cleveland's urban core.

Fig. 1. Terminal Tower, Cleveland, by Graham, Anderson, Probst & White, 1927.

THE GROUP PLAN OF 1903

At the turn of the twentieth century, downtown Cleveland was an ensemble of commercial buildings, offices, and manufacturing spaces, developed largely through land speculation, as formal city planning was still emerging as a profession. To the city's civic leaders, downtown was disorganized and incoherent and lacked imposing spaces and buildings. As a result, local power brokers, including elected officials and wealthy residents, were spurred to rebuild part of downtown, with the aim of matching the grandeur of other world cities. This effort was known as the Group Plan.

The first step was convincing the Ohio legislature to authorize Governor George K. Nash to establish the Group Plan Commission, which was created in 1902. With input from the city's leaders, the governor selected an impressive trio to lead the new endeavor: Daniel Burnham, the prominent Chicago-based architect behind the 1893 World's Columbian Exposition; Arnold Brunner, a New York–based architect who had trained at MIT and worked under George B. Post; and the distinguished New York architect John Carrère, who had trained at the École des Beaux-Arts in Paris. The overall goal was to elevate Cleveland's public buildings and civic spaces, connect to the city's existing Public Square, and establish a monumental gateway to the city from the Lake Erie waterfront.

A new federal building was already planned, just off the northeast corner of Public Square. The Commission included the federal building as a part of the Group Plan, thus partially driving decision-making about the location for a new civic center. As detailed in a speech given by Brunner at the Eighth National Conference on City

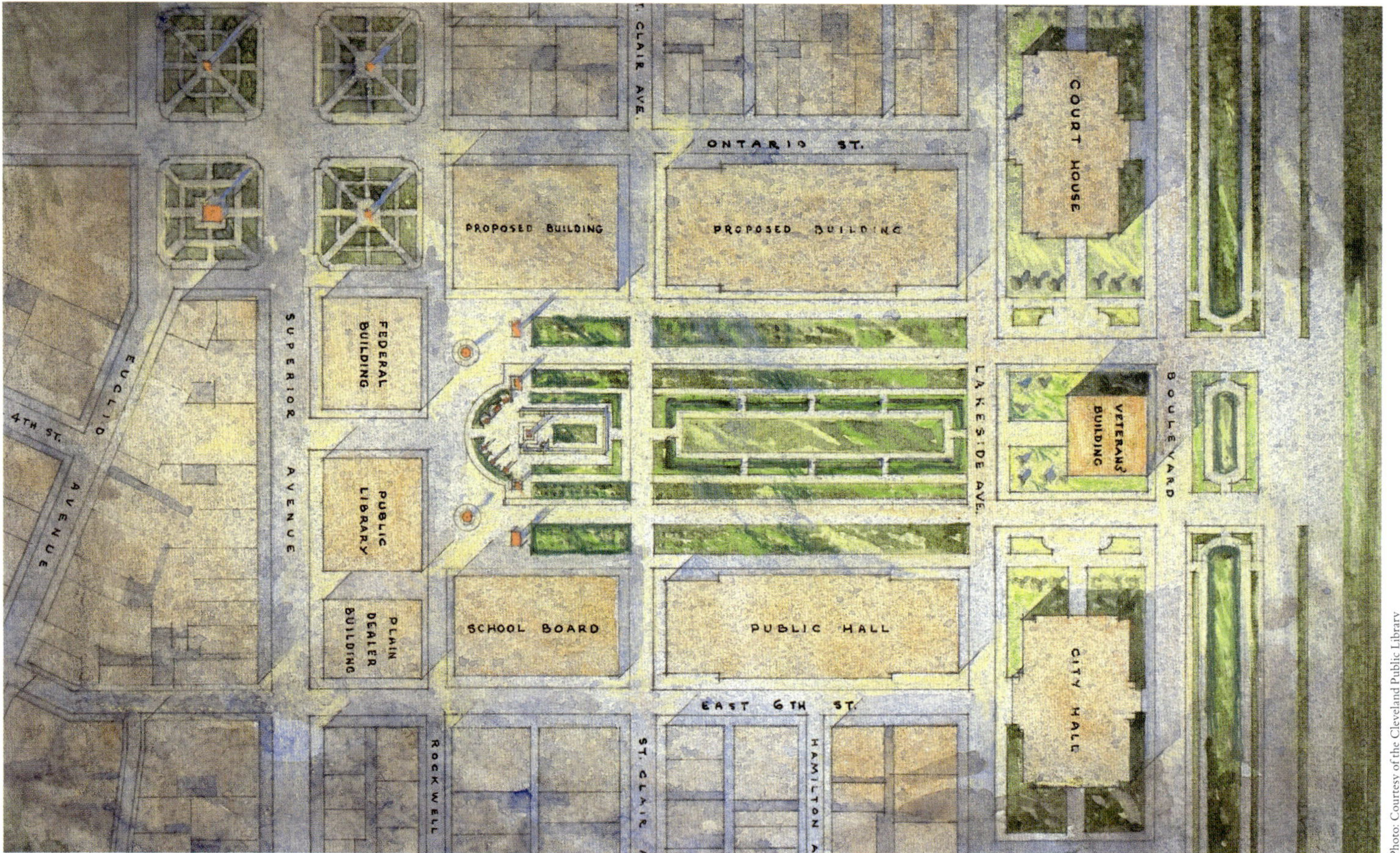

Photo: Courtesy of the Cleveland Public Library

Fig. 2. Group Plan for Cleveland by Daniel Burnham, 1904.

Planning in Cleveland in 1916, this area of downtown was underdeveloped and in poor condition, making it inexpensive for the city to purchase the land and demolish the existing buildings. The Group Plan Commission determined that planning efforts for a new city hall, county courthouse, public library, and rail station could all be incorporated into the new civic center. The decision to site the Group Plan along Lake Erie also followed prior advocacy on the part of Cleveland's Chamber of Commerce to better utilize the lakefront as public and civic space.

The Commission's plan, accepted by Cleveland's mayor in 1903, called for a three-part central Mall, with classically designed buildings providing enclosure and formality (fig. 2). Seven buildings were planned, featuring uniform height, massing, and Beaux-Arts architecture. According to Brunner, the Commission was inspired by the scale, mass, and layout of Paris's Place de la Concorde. The most challenging aspects were the siting, design, and logistics of the proposed railroad station enclosing the north end of the Mall. Brunner noted that the design of the station and the physical connection between the Mall and Lake Erie, which sat at a lower elevation, needed further study. During the planning process, there were concerns that the entire ensemble was too large and too costly, and some critics suggested that commercial, rather than public buildings, should flank the Mall. These were rejected by the city and, according to Brunner's reflections, popular sentiment.

EARLY GROUP PLAN BUILDINGS

The first of the Group Plan structures, and one of the most complete embodiments of Beaux-Arts architectural principles in Ohio, was the Federal Building and U.S. Post Office (opened 1910; fig. 3). The five-story building, designed by Brunner at the southwest corner of the Mall, was clad in granite, with arched windows topped with carved keystones at the rusticated ground level. Corinthian columns and pilasters standing 42 feet tall define the upper bays. On the exterior, Daniel Chester French, designer of the statue of Abraham Lincoln at the

Photo: Kenneth Grant/Alamy Stock Photo

Fig. 3. Federal Building and U.S. Post Office (now the Howard M. Metzenbaum U.S. Courthouse), Cleveland, 1910, by Arnold Brunner.

Lincoln Memorial, created neoclassical sculptures, while the interior features murals by Frederick Crowninshield.

The Federal Building was followed by the Cuyahoga County Courthouse (1912), which was the fifth iteration of a county courthouse in downtown Cleveland, and Cleveland City Hall (1916), flanking the north end of the Group Plan. The courthouse, designed by the local architecture firm Lehman & Schmitt, with Charles Morris (an École des Beaux-Arts alumnus) as chief designer, is an architecturally stunning building that recalls a classical temple motif on its granite exterior. Charles Schweinfurth, one of Cleveland's most prolific architects, designed the interior with a vaulted three-story central court featuring marble Ionic columns and a balustraded mezzanine. Cleveland architect J. Milton Dyer designed Cleveland City Hall as a near twin of the county courthouse.

By the early 1930s, the Group Plan had transformed this part of Cleveland, which now included Public Auditorium (1922), Cleveland Public Library (1926), and the Board of Education (1931). The clean lines, marble and granite finishes, and classical influences stood in stark contrast to the heavy industry and the disordered industrial urban landscape (fig. 6). As Brunner had projected in his 1916 speech on the Group Plan's design, "The Civic Centre is where the city speaks to us, where it asserts itself. Here the streets meet and agree to submit to regulation. They resolve themselves into some regular form, the buildings stop swearing at each other, competition is forgotten, individuals are no longer rivals—they are all citizens. Petty struggles for prominence, small successes and failures disappear. Here the citizens assume their rights and duties and here civic pride is born."

PUBLIC SQUARE

Public Square had been laid out in 1796 and modeled after New England's traditional town commons. The southeast corner of the Square remained distinguished by the Soldiers' and Sailors' Monument, which had been designed in 1894 by local architect Levi Scofield to pay tribute to Clevelanders who fought in the Civil War. The

Photo: Courtesy of the Cleveland Public Library

Fig. 4. Public Square, c. 1925, with the Soldiers' and Sailors' Monument by Levi Scofield, 1894.

central column, 125 feet tall and seven feet in diameter, rests atop a granite base with an interior memorial room. Cast-bronze sculptures and an esplanade surround the base, raised above Public Square's ground level in the tradition of elevated monuments (fig. 4). When the Group Plan's Federal Building was constructed at the northeast corner of Public Square, the magnificent Soldiers' and Sailors' Monument provided a balancing effect, anchoring the southern end of the square.

The Group Plan had called for a railroad station at the northern terminus of the Mall as a monumental gateway, leading those arriving to the city along the grand Mall and into the core of the commercial city via Public Square. In the vision of the Group Plan Commission, Public Square was the connective urban fabric between the city's new gateway and Cleveland's downtown commercial core. That all changed with the development of the massive Union Terminal complex (1922–31) at the southwest corner of Public Square. The Van Sweringen brothers, local developers of the tony streetcar suburb of Shaker Heights, purchased multiple blocks of land and demolished more than 1,000 buildings to build Union Terminal as a passenger rail connection to Shaker Heights. When constructed, the fifty-two-story Terminal Tower (Graham, Anderson, Probst & White, 1927) was the nation's tallest building outside of New York City (fig. 1). Union Terminal became Cleveland's primary passenger rail station, increasing Public Square's prominence and disrupting Burnham, Brunner, and Carrère's vision for the Group Plan's gateway rail station. Public Square, more intimate than the Mall, was surrounded by active land uses (churches, banks, department stores), fostering natural vitality and pedestrian activity. People traveling by rail now entered the city via Union Terminal and Public Square, typically headed east on Euclid Avenue, and bypassed the Group Plan, tempering its civic importance.

EUCLID AVENUE

Euclid Avenue, Cleveland's primary east-west corridor, extends from the southeast corner of Public Square to University Circle and the eastern suburbs. By the turn of the twentieth century, Euclid Avenue from Public Square to East 9th Street was a bustling commercial center. Farther east, the verdant avenue housed the mansions of industrial titans, leading to the nickname "Millionaires' Row." The mansions were eclectic in style and included the Italianate Amasa Stone House (1857) and numerous Romanesque Revival homes designed by local architect Charles Schweinfurth. By the mid-twentieth century, most of the Millionaires' Row mansions had been demolished to make way for more commercial development, including offices, financial institutions, retail, and entertainment such as the Playhouse Square district.

Euclid Avenue's development rapidly intensified in the early twentieth century as the avenue became a showcase for notable buildings in the city. The iconic May Company department store (1915, 1931), designed by Daniel Burnham in the Chicago School style with a prominent white terra-cotta facade, served as a transition from Public Square to Euclid Avenue and complimented the nearby Group Plan buildings. One of the nation's oldest indoor shopping halls, the Cleveland Arcade (1890), by George H. Smith and John Eisenmann, was executed in a Richardsonian Romanesque style on the exterior, which contrasted with the building's 300-foot iron and glass ceiling that floods the interior with light (fig. 5). The Citizens Bank building (1903), designed by the leading Cleveland-based architectural firm Hubbell & Benes, featured a classically inspired portico with thirty-foot-tall Doric columns and a classical entablature and pediment. George B. Post & Sons, architects of the New York Stock Exchange, designed the Cleveland Trust Company (1905–08) in the neoclassical style at the corner of East 9th Street and Euclid Avenue, with dual entrances reminiscent of Greek temple structures. The interior boasted thirteen murals by Francis D. Millet, who also worked on the 1893 World's Columbian Exposition and designed murals for Boston's Trinity Church. The imposing Union Trust building (Graham, Anderson, Probst & White, 1923) at East 9th and Euclid featured neoclassical influences, including three-story Ionic columns and a barrel-vaulted ceiling and skylights, punctuated with Corinthian columns and decorative murals by Jules Guérin, designer of the murals at the Lincoln Memorial in Washington, DC.

Photo: artaxerxes_longhand/Alamy Stock Photo

Fig. 5. Cleveland Arcade, interior, by George H. Smith and John Eisenmann, 1890

UNIVERSITY CIRCLE

Euclid Avenue connects downtown Cleveland to University Circle, a cluster of arts, cultural, educational, and medical institutions. The seeds of University Circle date to one of Cleveland's wealthiest industrialists and philanthropists, Jeptha Wade, who made his fortune as the developer of telegraph lines and held interests in railroad companies, banks, and steel manufacturing. Wade owned a large tract of land on the eastern edge of the city and, in the 1870s, developed a vision for using a portion of his tract as a public park. In 1882, he donated part of his land to the City of Cleveland, which named the area Wade Park.

Wade's donation stipulated that the park include a public art gallery. In 1916, the Cleveland Museum of Art, designed by Hubbell & Benes, fulfilled that directive. The building occupies one of University Circle's most prominent sites, elevated above Wade Lagoon and overlooking both Euclid Avenue and Wade Park (now called Wade Oval). Made of white Georgian marble, the neoclassical building features a central portico with Ionic columns (fig. 7). After completing the museum building, Hubbell & Benes created a plan calling for the creation of a cultural district in the area. In contrast to the Group Plan, the plan for University Circle was not formally adopted by the city, and subsequent development varied considerably. Yet, the cultural district concept took root even as piecemeal planning occurred over subsequent decades. The construction of Severance Hall (1931), designed by Walker & Weeks, provided a long-sought permanent home for the Cleveland Orchestra and combined neoclassical elements with Egyptian Revival and Art Deco influences (see p. 16). Other institutions moved into the growing cultural district that included the Cleveland Garden Center (predecessor of the Cleveland Botanical Garden), the Western Reserve Historical Society, and the Cleveland Museum of Natural History.

University Circle also emerged as Cleveland's educational district. In addition to donating the park to the city, Wade provided land for Western Reserve University and was involved with creating the Case School of Applied Science in 1880. In 1883, Western Reserve University relocated from Hudson, Ohio (30 miles south), to University Circle;

Photo: Courtesy of the Cleveland Public Library

Fig. 6. Cleveland Mall, with Group Plan buildings, c. 1930.

in 1885, the Case School of Applied Science moved to the district from downtown. (The two institutions merged in 1967 into Case Western Reserve University.) Related medical institutions moved to University Circle, eventually leading to both University Hospital and the Cleveland Clinic establishing their core facilities in the district. While University Circle's educational and medical institutions exhibit a variety of architectural styles—evidencing their evolution and continued growth and expansion over time—there are vestiges of early-twentieth-century classical architecture in spaces like the former Temple-Tifereth Israel building (by Charles R. Greco, 1924) on the Case Western Reserve campus—a heptagonal, Byzantine-inspired structure featuring a prominent gold dome and now adaptively reused as a performing arts center.

A CONTEMPORARY REBIRTH FOR CLEVELAND'S URBAN LANDSCAPES

The monumental landscapes of the Group Plan, Public Square, Euclid Avenue, and University Circle maintained their hold as defining elements of Cleveland's image in the second half of the twentieth century. But they also began to reflect the city's declining prominence by the mid-twentieth century as a period of decades-long economic and population contraction set in.

While the Group Plan remains one of the nation's most intact City Beautiful developments, it was not fully realized and did not live up to expectations. The plan had called for seven classically designed civic buildings and a railroad station to put Cleveland on par with the world's great cities. By the end of the 1920s, only six of the buildings had been completed, and the railroad station was never built. In 1916, Brunner had noted concerns about the project's scale, but the Mall's size was deemed ideal to convey monumentality, reflect Cleveland's prominence, and serve the city's large population—just under 800,000 in 1920. However, the Mall's vast scale and lack of street-level uses hindered walkability and urban vitality. The Group Plan was realized during the peak of Cleveland's industrial might and, while the city continued to grow until 1950, subsequent decades of suburbanization and population decline meant fewer people in need of downtown open space, so the Mall was largely underutilized.

Cleveland's population peaked in 1950, with 914,808 residents, before declining by nearly 60 percent over the next seven decades. Deindustrialization took hold by the 1970s, punctuated by the closing of many steel plants in northeast Ohio. Amid decline and strained municipal coffers, the iconic Group Plan has remained an active public space. The city recognized the importance of the Group Plan buildings via local preservation protections. When the Cleveland Landmarks Commission formed in the early 1970s, the first locally protected building was City Hall, reflecting both local government leadership in preservation, the enduring legacy of the Group Plan, and the lasting influence of classical architecture. In the twenty-first century, its spatial framework has been preserved and enhanced with a new hotel, a convention center, and reconfigured open space.

Public Square continues to evolve to meet the needs of the city, even as the number of daily visitors entering via Union Terminal declines. In the 1980s and '90s, some of the oldest

Photo: Ian Dagnall/Alamy Stock Photo

Fig. 7. Cleveland Museum of Art by Hubbell & Benes, 1916.

buildings around the Square were demolished to make way for new skyscrapers, while the Union Terminal complex was redesigned as a downtown mall and is now being adaptively reused and reactivated. James Corner Field Operations and Cleveland-based LAND Studio redesigned Public Square in 2016, notably retaining the Soldiers' and Sailors' Monument in its original location.

Along Euclid Avenue, adaptive reuse has brought life back to this historic corridor. In 2014, the Cleveland Trust building was converted into commercial space, while preserving its magnificent interior detailing and classical exterior facade. A $270-million renovation of the Union Trust building includes apartments, a hotel, offices, retail, restaurants, and event facilities. Playhouse Square was on the brink of demolition in the 1970s, but after decades of restoration it is now one of the largest theater districts in the nation. The renovation of Euclid Avenue's historic fabric also paved the way for new construction.

University Circle's classical buildings and monumental landscapes are a testament to the enduring legacy of Cleveland's built environment. The attractive force of these historic institutions and their park-like setting, along with the prominence of Case Western Reserve University, the Cleveland Clinic, and other entities, has served as an anchor for contemporary reinvestment. In University Circle, new buildings have been developed, and historic buildings—including the Cleveland Museum of Art—have been expanded. Yet, the landmark classical motifs that laid the groundwork for the district's success still stand, giving the area definition and a sense of orientation, providing the foundation for ongoing investments and growth as the city's arts and cultural center.

Cleveland's monumental landscapes demonstrate powerful longevity and convey a strong sense of place and stability, even as the city has faced decades of decline and lost much of its economic dominance. Revitalization remains grounded in the urban spaces and public amenities created during the industrial era when the city's leaders and wealthy elites created monumental buildings and landscapes, often with classical influences. When demolition ravaged the urban landscape, many of these monumental spaces survived, which is testament to their beauty, function, and permanence in the urban landscape.

Urban leaders in Cleveland have tried myriad projects, investments, and strategies to spur reinvestment. No single policy directly protects the city's monumental landscapes. Local preservation protections exist, but many historic buildings have still fallen to the wrecking ball. Yet, there is inherent meaning and value in spaces like the Group Plan, Public Square, Euclid Avenue, and University Circle. They are compelling landmark spaces because of their purpose, architecture, location, and place in public memory. Monumental landscapes endure because they are valued beyond real estate or economic metrics. It may not be possible to fully measure or capture this value, but it can be seen in the ability of these spaces to attract and catalyze investment, hold a place in the city's public image, and anchor urban rebirth.

Stephanie Ryberg-Webster is Professor of Urban Affairs at the Maxine Goodman Levin School of Urban Affairs of Cleveland State University's Levin College of Public Affairs and Education. She is the author of *Preserving the Vanishing City: Historic Preservation amid Urban Decline in Cleveland, Ohio* (Temple University Press, 2023) and the co-editor of *Legacy Cities: Continuity and Change amid Decline and Revival* (University of Pittsburgh Press, 2019).

Thomas W. Hilde is Assistant Professor of Urban Planning at Cleveland State University's Levin College of Public Affairs and Education. His work also addresses the distinct challenges of U.S. legacy cities, contributing innovative approaches that bridge scholarship and practice.

MARIEMONT HIGH SCHOOL

FOUR LANDMARK OHIO SUBURBS

ANNE DELANO STEINERT

As industrialization took hold in the nineteenth century, Ohio's urban residents, like those throughout the nation, began looking for ways to dodge the pollution and crowding that factory-based production brought to American cities. The first to escape were those whose wealth provided access to private transportation.[1] In industrializing Cincinnati, this meant that wealthy industrialists moved up the hillsides to found rural villages like Clifton and Avondale.[2] In Cleveland, the escapees coalesced along a single spine, Euclid Avenue, eventually forming a Millionaires' Row of extreme opulence.[3] The appeal of these idyllic enclaves and those that followed began a cycle of suburban development expanding ever farther from the urban core. This can be seen by tracing the evolution of land use in four planned suburban Ohio towns: Glendale, Mariemont, Shaker Heights, and Greenhills.

SUBURBAN PRECURSORS

The first homes that affluent transplants built outside Ohio's cities conveyed the desire to differentiate rural and urban life, embodying Enlightenment ideals about beauty, nature, and the sublime expressed in the Picturesque movement. These ideas first found their way into the United States through the rural cemetery.[4]

As contagious diseases like cholera became an increasing concern for urban Americans, rural cemeteries developed outside urban centers, often with access by rail. These cemeteries, including Boston's Mount Auburn (1831), Cincinnati's Spring Grove (1844), and countless others, employed curving roads, taking visitors deep into a visually appealing park-like setting, and showed wealthy urbanites that it was possible to reclaim the peace and healthful promise of nature within reach of the city.[5]

These cemeteries were the earliest physical embodiment of treatises like Edmund Burke's *A Philosophical Enquiry into the Origin of Our Ideas of the Sublime and Beautiful* (1757) or Uvedale Price's *Essay on the Picturesque, as Compared with the Sublime and the Beautiful* (1794).[6] Such texts inspired architect Alexander Jackson Davis, his early partner Ithiel Towne, his later collaborator landscape designer Andrew Jackson Downing, and landscape architect Frederick Law Olmsted, who integrated these ideas into his designs for New York's Central Park and numerous other parks, cemeteries, and suburbs.[7] Together, these men set the fashion for a generation of prosperous Americans in both architecture and town planning, and their published works became the plan books of the age. They designed both buildings and towns based on formal classical principles adapted to American life and landscapes.[8]

In Cincinnati, the early influence of these designers appeared in landscaped Gothic "cottages" like A. H. Ernst's Scarlet Oaks in Clifton and Samuel Cloon's residence on Reading Road in Avondale, both published in a short-lived gentleman's journal called *Western Horticultural Review*.[9] The similarities to designs published by Davis and Downing are striking, but what is more compelling is the text accompanying the 1851 description of Cloon's home: "Mr. Cloon is anxious to diminish his cares, he is also willing to curtail the extent of his farm, by selling some portions for building sites, for which purpose much of his land is admirably suited. So that we may expect, in a few years, to see a delightful rural village springing up around him; and Clinton Farm will have to yield to 'Clinton Center.'"[10] Cloon was looking to subdivide his land and create a community of like-minded urban escapees.

Fig. 1. Old Mariemont High School, Mariemont, by E. C. Landberg, 1935–39.

Photo: Warren LeMay

Photo: Anne Delano Steinert

Fig. 2. Britton Roberts House, Glendale, built 1855.

A few months earlier, the same publication carried a short description of William S. Chapman's home at Linwood, offering a glimpse into the design of Ohio's earliest suburbs: "Mr. Chapman is about to appropriate his grounds into a SUBURBAN VILLAGE, an idea which is new to us in the West, but which is said to have been successfully carried out in other places."[11] The plan was for Chapman to subdivide housing lots along his long carriage drive and enclose his lawn as a public garden. As early as the 1850s, large estates began giving way to attractive residential subdivisions designed to facilitate flight from the woes of city life.

Well before the automobile age, urbanites felt the pull of the suburbs. Early Cincinnati visitor Alexis de Tocqueville wrote a letter home to his mother in 1831 in which he portrayed Cincinnati as a place where "[e]verything is jarring, outlandish; nothing has yet found a secure place . . . a completely novel scene; everything about it expresses hectic growth; lovely houses and cottages; freshly paved, imperfectly aligned streets encumbered with building materials; unnamed squares; unnumbered houses; in short, the sketch of a city rather than a city."[12] This hectic pace was already pushing the wealthy up to the hillsides.

GLENDALE

The ability to move out of the city was closely connected to transportation technology, and though de Tocqueville arrived in Cincinnati by steamboat, other options soon made suburban life more attainable. The arrival of railroads in the decades before the Civil War facilitated suburban growth. Cincinnati was the sixth-largest city in the nation in the 1840 and 1850 censuses, after New York, Baltimore, Boston, Philadelphia, and New Orleans.[13] It was a dense, dirty, industrial hub where river and rail systems met. A logical step in residential development was the nation's first planned railroad suburb.[14]

Located fifteen miles outside of Cincinnati, the village of Glendale is generally held to be America's earliest planned suburb.[15] Planned in 1851 and incorporated in 1855, it was clearly designed based on the principles of the Picturesque movement.[16] Prominent businessmen joined together to found the suburban enclave along the line of the Cincinnati and Dayton Railroad. They compiled about 600 acres and hired Cincinnati city engineer Robert C. Phillips to lay out a plan for the village.[17] Building lots were offered for sale, and profits were used to lay out the streets and other civic amenities (fig. 3).[18] Phillips's design featured Downingesque curvilinear streets set within varied and picturesque topographical features emphasizing natural vistas framed by formal elements, shifting as one moved through the landscape—features previously used only in cemeteries and elite private estates.

An 1870 publication made note of the comprehensive and picturesque nature of the village, stating: "Glendale should rather be considered as a whole than in detail. There are no palatial mansions, no extensive lawns, no long, sweeping graveled drives, such as the visitor sees in some other suburbs. It is rather a collection of beautiful homes, with ample grounds and profuse shrubbery, approached by circuitous avenues, and distinguished for the air of comfort and retirement that everywhere prevails . . . There are no towering hills nor immense stretches of valley; but quiet landscapes say to fatigued limbs and wearied minds, 'Here is rest.'"[19]

Photo: Anne Delano Steinert

Fig. 3. Glendale Village Hall and Fire Station, by Samuel Hannaford, 1875.

Those "beautiful homes" varied widely in style and materials but shared deep setbacks and large lawns that created an unmistakable park-like character merging individual lots into the larger village plan (fig. 2). Glendale's 1855 plat includes two football-shaped parks, and a jigsaw puzzle of irregular lots.

Though Downing clearly had an influence on the exterior appearance of this community, moral reformers like Catharine Beecher influenced interior features. Beecher, who spent some of her most productive years in Cincinnati's then-rural Walnut Hills neighborhood, published her ideas on "domestic economy" and advocated for interior features such as central hearths and cheerful, efficient kitchens to situate mothers at the center of family life and facilitate their work as domestic and moral exemplars.[20] The type of calm, orderly, Christian household advocated by the immensely influential Beecher was virtually impossible surrounded by the alluring rush and temptations of city life.

Scheduled trains ran between Cincinnati and Glendale with six departures in each direction per day, so the distance was surmountable, but effectively insulated Glendale from the hurly-burly of urban life.[21] An early description noted that the distance "saves its inhabitants from visitors that would otherwise . . . swarm in their streets and, build up beer and wine gardens that would rob them of their quiet, and soon convert Glendale into quite another community."[22]

As if predicting the homogeneity of postwar white flight, local historian and booster Sidney Maxwell described a class-based "cement" to life in Glendale in 1869 this way: "The great advantage about Glendale is that it is a complete community. Too far removed from the city to depend upon it for general society or amusement, it becomes a society itself, bound together as well by common necessity and the intimate friendships that frequent intercourse fosters . . . [and] finds, to some extent, a common cement in similar education and tastes. The inhabitants are generally intelligent and refined, and their influence is expended on such objects as promote the public good."[23] Glendale laid a foundation for suburban development in Ohio and across the country, although it would take several decades to popularize the trend.

Photo: Anne Delano Steinert

Fig. 4. Denny Place residence, Mariemont, by Howe & Manning, 1924.

MARIEMONT

Nearly seventy years after Glendale's incorporation, a very different model suburb was built on the east side of Cincinnati. As cities grew and urban conditions worsened, benevolent investors sought ways to provide more dignified housing for the working class. In Cincinnati this was especially urgent. In their 1903 study of tenement conditions nationwide, *The Tenement House Problem*, Robert DeForest and Lawrence Veiller revealed the extent of the Queen City's housing predicament: "Cincinnati, with a population of 325,902, after New York and Boston, has the worst housing conditions of any city in America."[24] In 1921, Cincinnati's Better Housing League reported that 70 percent of the 1,705 tenement buildings they surveyed relied on outdoor toilet facilities and that only 80 bathtubs existed across all the buildings.[25] There were few tested solutions to this crisis, but one stood out.

British designer Ebenezer Howard's 1898 *To-Morrow: A Peaceful Path to Real Reform*, later republished under the more well-known title *Garden Cities of To-Morrow*, innovated a novel solution to urban struggles in self-sustaining garden cities. Using compelling text and diagrams, Howard called for ample green space, small individual homes, transportation systems, industry, and community amenities to be grouped together into a series of planned communities. His "Diagram No. 7" presented a plan for 250,000, to be housed in a central city ringed by six smaller garden cities in a "group of slumless smokeless cities."[26] Each enclave was to occupy 1,000 acres and be surrounded by a 5,000-acre protective band of farms, forests, and parks to limit growth and maintain residents' connection to nature. Howard's ideas were designed to eventually pay for themselves but required ambitious initial investments. Howard himself undertook the construction of two towns, Letchworth and Welwyn, both in Hertfordshire, north of London, which served as a model for one Cincinnati philanthropist, Mary Emery.[27]

Emery, the widow of candle manufacturer and real estate developer Thomas J. Emery, invested much of her fortune in the construction of Mariemont, ten miles east of Cincinnati, based on Howard's ideas. In Mariemont, Emery attempted to appropriate features of the usual upper-class suburbs to relieve the dreadful urban conditions of Cincinnati's working class and provide enrichment through life rooted in community and set in nature.[28]

Mariemont was designed by pioneering urban planner John Nolen, who believed profoundly in the power of the natural environment to uplift American workers. In Mariemont, Nolen gave primacy to the land's natural conditions, responding to topography to derive the town's form and plan. Though the final plan utilized rectilinear lots, it also employed broadly curving streets threaded between a series of diagonals that radiated from a central town square, all embedded within a series of large parks. Construction began in 1922, and the nucleus of the village was ready for occupancy in 1924.[29]

Mariemont offered a range of attractive housing options, including apartments, small town houses, and larger detached single-family homes, all built by the Mariemont Corporation.[30] Despite centralized development, the individual building designs vary, as the corporation

Fig. 5. Van Sweringen brothers' residence, Shaker Heights, Ohio, by H. T. Jeffrey, 1909–12; enlarged and renovated by Phillip Small, 1924.

deliberately employed many of the best local and national architectural talents. Buildings rely on similar massing, steeply pitched roofs, and a simple material palette to unify the village, while ranging from the heavy half-timbering of the Mariemont Inn, by Cincinnati firm Zettel & Rapp, to the humble homes of Denny Place, designed by pioneering women architects Lois Howe and Eleanor Manning (fig. 4). The Denny Place houses appear ordinary today, but these and others throughout the village were, in fact, models for now-ubiquitous small- to medium-sized American single-family homes constructed by speculative developers throughout the country through the 1950s.[31]

The village included a small but vital business district, schools, churches, and a range of recreational opportunities (fig. 1). Streetcars provided transit into downtown. The 1943 *WPA Guide* called Mariemont "an ideal community," designed with a philanthropic ideal to provide high-quality affordable housing for working-class residents, and "a complete town," including all amenities necessary so that residents could live there without relying on trips into the city.[32] Highlighting the beauty of the village, the *Guide* rhapsodized about the power lines, buried to avoid marring any views.[33]

Mariemont was a dreamlike community and exerted a powerful pull for many urban residents, but not all were welcome. Its population was controlled by restrictive covenants that expressly barred African American and Asian residents.[34] Buyers needed to be approved by the company and had to promise to resell their property back to the developer if they moved away, to keep the community white and exclude potential residents deemed undesirable.[35] Sadly, Mariemont did not achieve the desired level of affordability, so it was unable to serve its intended occupants and has remained a middle- and upper-middle class community since shortly after its inception.[36]

SHAKER HEIGHTS

Cleveland developed slowly, but by the 1890s it matured as an industrial powerhouse and moved up to the tenth-largest city in America.[37] As the new century approached, a string of eastern suburbs appeared, providing an exclusive retreat for those able to afford it. The most notable among these is Shaker Heights, where growth over forty years set a model for successful suburban planning, design, and marketing.

The brothers Oris and Mantis Van Sweringen, known as "the Vans," began purchasing real estate in what would

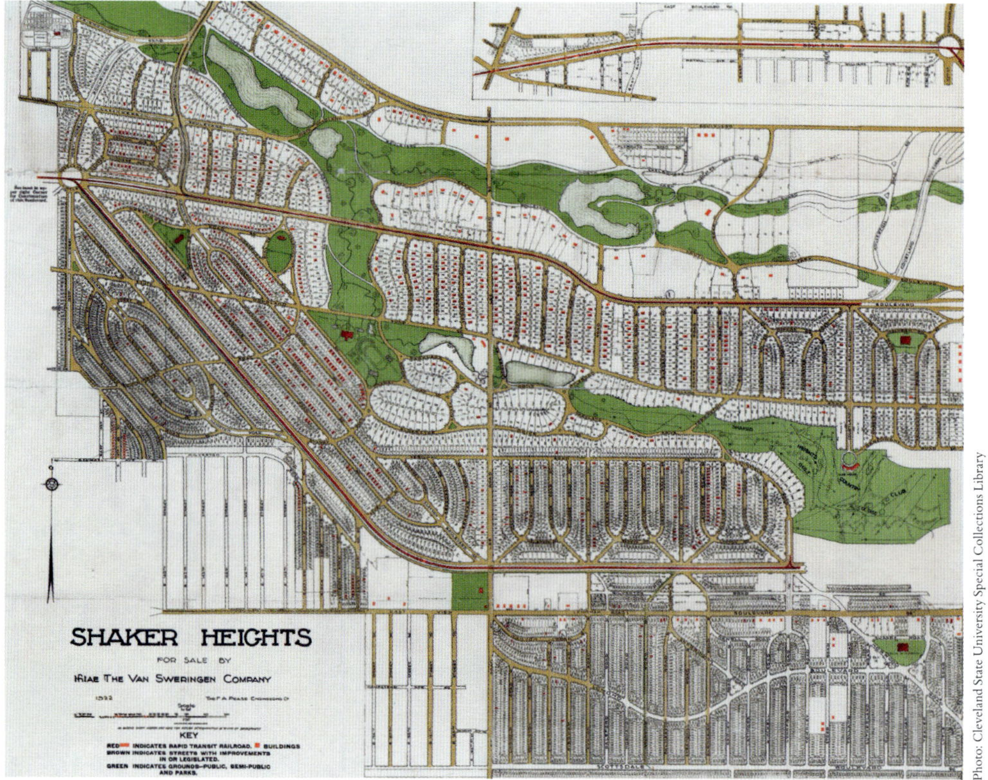

Photo: Cleveland State University Special Collections Library

Fig. 6. Map of Shaker Heights from the Van Sweringen Company's sales booklet, by F.A. Pease Engineering, 1922.

become Shaker Heights, in 1905, but it was not until they completed a dedicated streetcar line in the 1920s that their development gained traction (figs. 5, 6).[38] During the interwar period, not coincidentally concurrent with the Great Migration, upper-class Ohioans relocated to exclusive, streetcar-connected suburbs at a remarkable rate. In Shaker Heights the population boomed from 1,600 in 1920 to over 17,000 in 1930. Professional, white city dwellers used affordable mass transit and newly affordable private automobiles to leave city neighborhoods behind for the city's new arrivals.[39] While elements of city life, including a changing racial climate, pushed many families to move to the suburbs, Shaker Heights itself also beckoned city residents with spacious homes, racial and socioeconomic homogeneity, and the separation of residential and commercial functions. At the Cleveland border, a commercial development called Shaker Square served as a gateway to the community and provided essential commercial functions at a distance from residential areas.[40]

Designed by the F.A. Pease Engineering Company, Shaker Heights encompassed over 4,000 acres by 1920.[41] It combined a park-like setting with faster roads for automobiles, using boulevards for traffic and secondary curving streets to provide safety and break the whole into smaller neighborhoods. These neighborhoods grouped residents by class, with larger houses in one area and more modest homes in another, and, like Mariemont, provided access to community resources. The Van Sweringen brothers carefully regulated their town with restrictive covenants limiting housing styles, setbacks, colors, cost, and the race and religion of residents—the community was closed to African Americans and Jews until 1949.[42] The houses in Shaker Heights were designed individually though often based on demonstration homes designed by the Van Sweringens' architects. They vary stylistically but are unified by deep setbacks on broad lawns and exacting size and height requirements.

Beyond the size of the enterprise and the ferocity of its restrictions, Shaker Heights also innovated suburban promotion with an aggressive sales campaign that included huge newspaper ads, promotional signage, staged demonstration homes, and sales events.[43] Thanks to these innovations, lots sold quickly, and the restrictive covenants fulfilled the Vans' advertising promise to keep the community "free from commercial or social invasion."[44] The strategy was successful, and while the overextended Van Sweringens met with financial ruin during the Great Depression, Shaker Heights remains synonymous with privilege, beauty, and comfort even today.

GREENHILLS

As the Great Depression brought suffering across class during the 1930s, President Franklin Delano Roosevelt sought to relieve American workers by providing jobs and housing with a series of innovative New Deal Greenbelt Towns. Under the Resettlement Administration (RA), Roosevelt's advisor Rexford

Tugwell built a team of the nation's brightest planners, engineers, and architects to design self-sufficient garden cities rooted in the ideals of Ebenezer Howard and other planning exemplars.

Located 25 miles north of Cincinnati, Greenhills is one of three Greenbelt Towns designed and built by the RA. Though the towns were developed under the same federal program, each town had its own design team, and amenities differed based on the needs of their communities.[45] Greenbelt, Maryland, for example, included more apartment buildings to accommodate single people who might be commuting to Washington, DC, while Greendale, Wisconsin, consists of predominately single-family homes. Greenhills straddles the middle, featuring apartments, fourplex town homes, and detached single-family units. These houses also straddle stylistic lines, with a discordant pairing of Colonial Revival–style homes with others in the more modern International Style. Greenhills, like Mariemont, differed from most suburbs in that the developer, in this case the federal government, constructed the residential units.[46] Here, the government retained ownership and rented homes to residents it deemed worthy through a lengthy screening process, including income caps, designed to build a homogenous community of hardworking residents committed to family and community life.[47]

Though its housing was significant, Greenhills is most important for the innovations in its plan. The village was surrounded on all sides by a dense wooded greenbelt that protected it from unplanned growth. Within the village, the number of through streets was limited, and cul-de-sacs were used to control the volume of traffic on residential thoroughfares.[48] Blocks were large but contained an internal network of pedestrian walkways and underpasses, allowing children and families to travel throughout the village on foot, largely isolated from moving traffic. A K–12 school, community building and swimming pool, village green, volunteer fire department, and shopping plaza containing one of the area's first credit unions and a cooperative grocery store were the village's central gathering points (fig. 7).[49] Children who grew up in the early years of Greenhills remember it as an idyllic oasis of wholesome family life.[50]

Photo: Anne Delano Steinert

Fig. 7. Community Building, Greenhills, by Roland Wank, 1938.

WHAT COMES NEXT

Each of the four Ohio suburbs explored in this essay rests on the same values of connection to nature, walkability, and a sense of community among peers. Each is rooted in visionary leadership and investment. All are beautiful and landmarks in suburban history, yet they share one essential shortcoming. Their very existence has its roots in a desire to evade parts of city life, an anti-urbanism that still plagues the nation. Though many Americans today are choosing urban residences, maintenance of suburban ideas about personal space, quiet, parking, and homogeneity may be factors in pushing longtime, low-income urban residents out and irrevocably altering cities as they have been known for the past century. As Americans weather this shift, perhaps the most significant lesson from these four suburbs is that Ohio's designers and business leaders are creative and innovative problem solvers willing to take big risks—a lesson that may well create remedies for the complications of contemporary urban life. In today's shifting urban landscape, it is more important to imagine what Ohio can innovate next.

Anne Delano Steinert is Research Assistant Professor of History at the University of Cincinnati, where she also directs the Center for the City and serves as the Taft Research Center 2025–2028 Professor of Social Justice. Her grandparents, Anne and Stanley Steinert, were original residents of Greenhills, Ohio. As a public urban historian, she has curated numerous local exhibits and is currently working on a multi-site exhibition on the history of Cincinnati's Avondale neighborhood. She is also the founding board chair of the Over-the-Rhine Museum. Steinert holds a BA in historic preservation from Goucher College, an MS in historic preservation from Columbia University, and an MA and PhD in urban American history from the University of Cincinnati.

Notes

1. Sam Bass Warner Jr. *Streetcar Suburbs: The Process of Growth in Boston 1870–1900* (Cambridge, MA: Harvard University Press, 1962), vii–x.

2. Zane L. Miller, *Boss Cox's Cincinnati: Urban Politics in the Progressive Era* (New York: Oxford University Press, 1968), 5–8.

3. William Ganson Rose, *Cleveland: The Making of a City* (Cleveland, OH: The World Publishing Company, 1950), 361–68.

4. Blanche Linden-Ward, "The Greening of Cincinnati: Adolf Strauch's Legacy in Park Design," *Queen City Heritage* 51, no. 1 (Spring 1993): 20–21.

5. Blanche M. G. Linden, "Spring Grove: Celebrating 150 Years," *Queen City Heritage* 53, no. 1/2 (Spring/Summer 1995): 4–7.

6. Alexander Brey, "Alexander Jackson Davis," *History of Early American Landscape Design* (National Gallery of Art), https://heald.nga.gov/mediawiki/index.php/Alexander_Jackson_Davis, accessed July 15, 2025.

7. Roy Rosenzweig and Elizabeth Blackmar, *The Park and the People: A History of Central Park* (Ithaca, NY: Cornell University Press, 1992), 121–39.

8. Brey, "Alexander Jackson Davis."

9. *Western Horticultural Review* 1, no. 3 (December 1850): frontispiece; and no. 10 (July 1851): frontispiece. The magazine included a multi-part review of Downing's *Country* Houses published between January and May 1851. The Scarlet Oaks discussed here was replaced in 1867 by George Schoenberger's Scarlet Oaks mansion, which stands today.

10. "The Frontispiece," *Western Horticultural Review* 1, no. 10 (July 1851): 503.

11. "Cheap Houses–Sunburnt Bricks–Suburban Village" *Western Horticultural Review* 1, no. 6 (March 1851): 310.

12. Alexis de Tocqueville, quoted in Frederick Brown, ed. and transl., *Alexis de Toqueville: Letters from America* (New Haven, CT: Yale University Press, 2012), 242.

13. Campbell Gibson, "Population of the 100 Largest Cities and Other Urban Places in the United States: 1790 to 1990," U.S. Bureau of the Census, "Table 7: Population of the 100 Largest Urban Places 1840," and "Table 8: Population of the Largest Urban Places 1850," https://www.census.gov/library/working-papers/1998/demo/POP-twps0027.html, accessed July 20, 2025.

14. John Archer, "Country and City in the American Romantic Suburb," *Journal of the Society of Architectural Historians* 42, no. 2 (May 1983): 154.

15. Robert A.M. Stern, David Fishman, and Jacob Tilove, *Paradise Planned: The Garden Suburb and the Modern City* (New York: The Monacelli Press, 2013), 120.

16. Sidney Maxwell notes that the distance from Cincinnati was fifteen miles by rail and eleven miles by the Carthage Turnpike (today known as Vine Street and Springfield Pike). See Sidney Maxwell, *The Suburbs of Cincinnati: Sketches Historical and Descriptive* (Cincinnati, OH: George E. Stevens & Co., 1870), 96.

17. Stern, et al., *Paradise Planned*, 120.

18. S. B. Nelson and J. M. Runk, *History of Cincinnati and Hamilton County, Ohio* (Cincinnati, OH: S. B. Nelson Publishers, 1894), 437–38.

19. Maxwell, *Suburbs of Cincinnati*, 77–78.

20. Catharine Beecher, *A Treatise on Domestic Economy for the Use of Young Ladies at Home and at School Third Edition* (New York: Harper & Brothers, 1845), 318.

21. Maxwell, *Suburbs of Cincinnati*, 97.

22. Maxwell, *Suburbs of Cincinnati*, 96.

23. Maxwell, *Suburbs of Cincinnati*, 99.

24. Robert Weeks DeForest and Lawrence Veiller, eds., *The Tenement House Problem*, vol. 1 (New York: Macmillan & Co., 1903), 144.

25. *Housing Progress in Cincinnati* (Cincinnati, OH: Better Housing League, 1921), 12–13.

26. Ebenezer Howard, *To-Morrow: A Peaceful Path to Real Reform* (London: Swan, Sonnenschein & Co., 1898), fig. 7.

27. Bruce Stephenson, *John Nolen: Landscape Architect and City Planner* (Amherst, MA: Library of American Landscape History, 2021), 58–59, 161.

28. Stephenson, *John Nolen*, 161.

29. Stephenson, *John Nolen*, 161–69.

30. Bradley D. Cross, "'On a Business Basis': An American Garden City," *Planning Perspectives* 19 (January 2004): 70–71.

31. National Park Service, "National Historic Landmark Nomination, Village of Mariemont" (2007), 31.

32. WPA Writers' Program, *Cincinnati: A Guide to the Queen City and Its Neighbors* (Cincinnati, OH: City of Cincinnati, 1943), 484–85.

33. WPA Writers' Program, *Cincinnati,* 484.

34. National Park Service, "National Historic Landmark Nomination, Village of Mariemont," 31.

35. WPA Writer's Program, *Cincinnati,* 485.

36. Cross, "'On a Business Basis,'" 71–72.

37. William Ganson Rose, *Cleveland: The Making of a City* (Cleveland, OH: Cleveland World Publishing, 1950), 91, 500.

38. Cynthia Mills Richter, "Integrating the Suburban Dream: Shaker Heights Ohio" (PhD diss., University of Minnesota, 1999), 7.

39. Jon C. Teaford, *Cities of the Heartland: The Rise and Fall of the Industrial Midwest* (Bloomington: Indiana University Press, 1993), 205–6.

40. Stern et al., *Paradise Planned*, 177.

41. Stern et al., *Paradise Planned*, 175.

42. Richter, *Integrating the Suburban Dream*, 7–21.

43. John R. Stilgoe, *Borderland: Origins of the American Suburb, 1820–1939* (New Haven, CT: Yale University Press, 1988), 241.

44. *The Heritage of the Shakers* (Cleveland, OH: The Van Sweringen Company, 1923), 29.

45. Julie D. Turner, *Best Laid Plans: The Promises and Pitfalls of the New Deal Greenbelt Towns* (Cincinnati, OH: University of Cincinnati Press, 2022), 83–85.

46. Turner, *Best Laid Plans*, 179–85.

47. Robert B. Fairbanks, "Greenhills: Model for Metropolitan Development," *Queen City Heritage* 48, no. 4 (Fall 1990): 9–10.

48. Rita Walsh, "Greenhills Historic District," Hamilton County, Ohio. National Register of Historic Places Inventory-Nomination Form, 1988. National Park Service, U.S. Department of the Interior, Washington, DC, 4.

49. Fairbanks, "Greenhills," 6–8.

50. Interview with Louis H. Steinert, June 1, 2025.

PROFESSIONAL PORTFOLIO

Additional images of work in the Professional Portfolio can be found at classicist.org/portfolios

Photo: Eric Piasecki

Arts and Crafts Residence, Hunting Valley
Peter Pennoyer Architects

Photo: Richard Mandelkorn

Western Reserve Residence, Gates Mills
William H. Childs, Jr. & Associates

Photo: Andrew Frasz

Residence, Chagrin Falls
Ferguson & Shamamian Architects

Photo: Andrew Frasz

Barn, Chagrin Falls
Ferguson & Shamamian Architects

Photo: Eric Piasecki

Rowdy Meadow, Hunting Valley
Peter Pennoyer Architects

Photo: Christian James Photo

David Cutler Conservatory, Hopewell Farm, Middlefield
Kawalek Architects

Photo: Richard Mandelkorn

"Pennsylvania" Stone House, Hunting Valley
William H. Childs, Jr. & Associates

Photo: Chris Rucinski

Lake Erie Country House, Huron
Patrick Ahearn Architect

Photo: Richard Mandelkorn

English Manor, Hunting Valley
William H. Childs, Jr. & Associates

Photo: Tony Paskevich, Architect

Marous House addition, Waite Hill
Paskevich & Associates

Photo: Eric Piasecki

Guest Cottage, Northern Ohio
Ferguson & Shamamian Architects

Photo: Alexander Abejuela

Neighborhood Launch (Gay and Fourth Streets), Columbus
The Jones Studio

Photo: Alexander Abejuela

Neighborhood Launch (Gay and Fourth Streets), Columbus
The Jones Studio

Photo: Nicholas Frederick

Cliff Road Residence, Catawba Island
Daniel Frederick Architects

Photo: Howard Doughty

Brainard Terrace Row Houses, Ohio City, Cleveland (rehabilitation of 1880s row)
The D.H. Ellison Co.

Photo: Anthony Catania

Union Village Bedel Street Townhouses, Lebanon
Michael Watkins Architect and Architects Associated

Photo: David Watkins

Union Village Commercial Building, Lebanon
Michael Watkins Architect and Phoenix Architecture

Photo: Cory Klein Photography

Topiary Park Crossing, Columbus
Moody Nolan

Photo: Snappy George Photography

Sacred Hearts Church, Cardington
William Heyer Architect

Photo: Paul Kelley

The Gramercy, Bexley
The Jones Studio

Photo: David Meleca Architects

The Cap at Union Station, Columbus
David Meleca (Moody Nolan)

Photo: © Brad Feinknopf

Hamilton Hall, The Ohio State University, Columbus, addition
RAMSA (Robert A.M. Stern Architects)

Photo: Francis Dzikowski/OTTO

Postle Hall, The Ohio State University, Columbus, addition
RAMSA (Robert A.M. Stern Architects)

Photo: Magnus Lindqvist/GLINTstudios

Cincinnati Music Hall, Cincinnati (restoration of 1878 building by Samuel Hannaford)
PWWG Architects

Photo: Jeff Goldberg, Esto Photographics

The Carlisle Building, Chillicothe (renovation and repurposing of 1885 building)
Schooley Caldwell

Photo: Kevin G Reeves

Ohio Theatre Lobby, Cleveland (re-creation of 1921 lobby by Thomas Lamb, destroyed by fire in 1964)
DLR Group

Photo: David Ellison

Sheoga Hardwood Flooring Co. (remodeling of 1980s building), Middlefield
The D.H. Ellison Co.

Photo: William Heyer

Tina & Dale Knobel Pavilion, Robbins Hunter Museum, Granville
William Heyer Architect

ACADEMIC PORTFOLIO

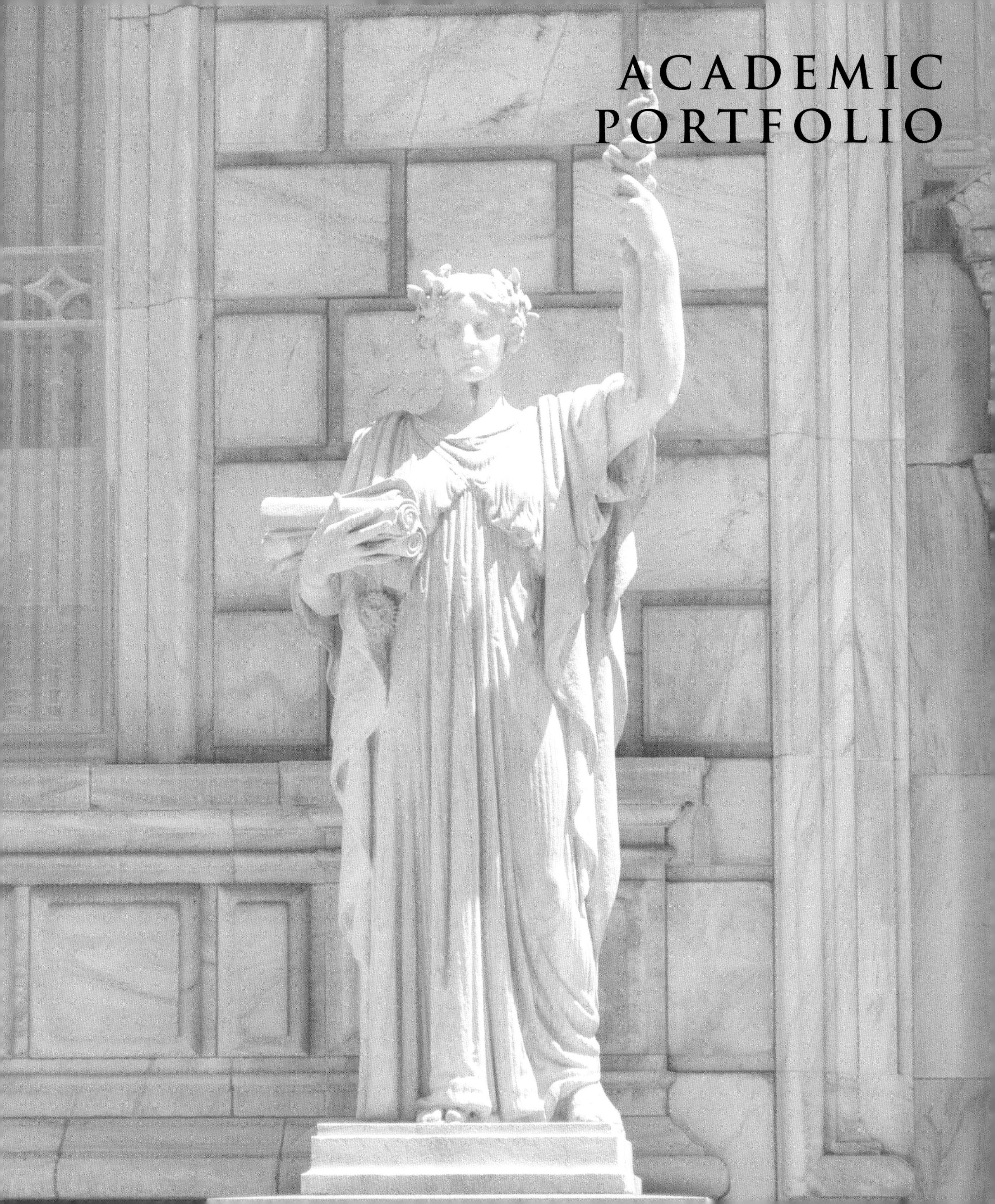

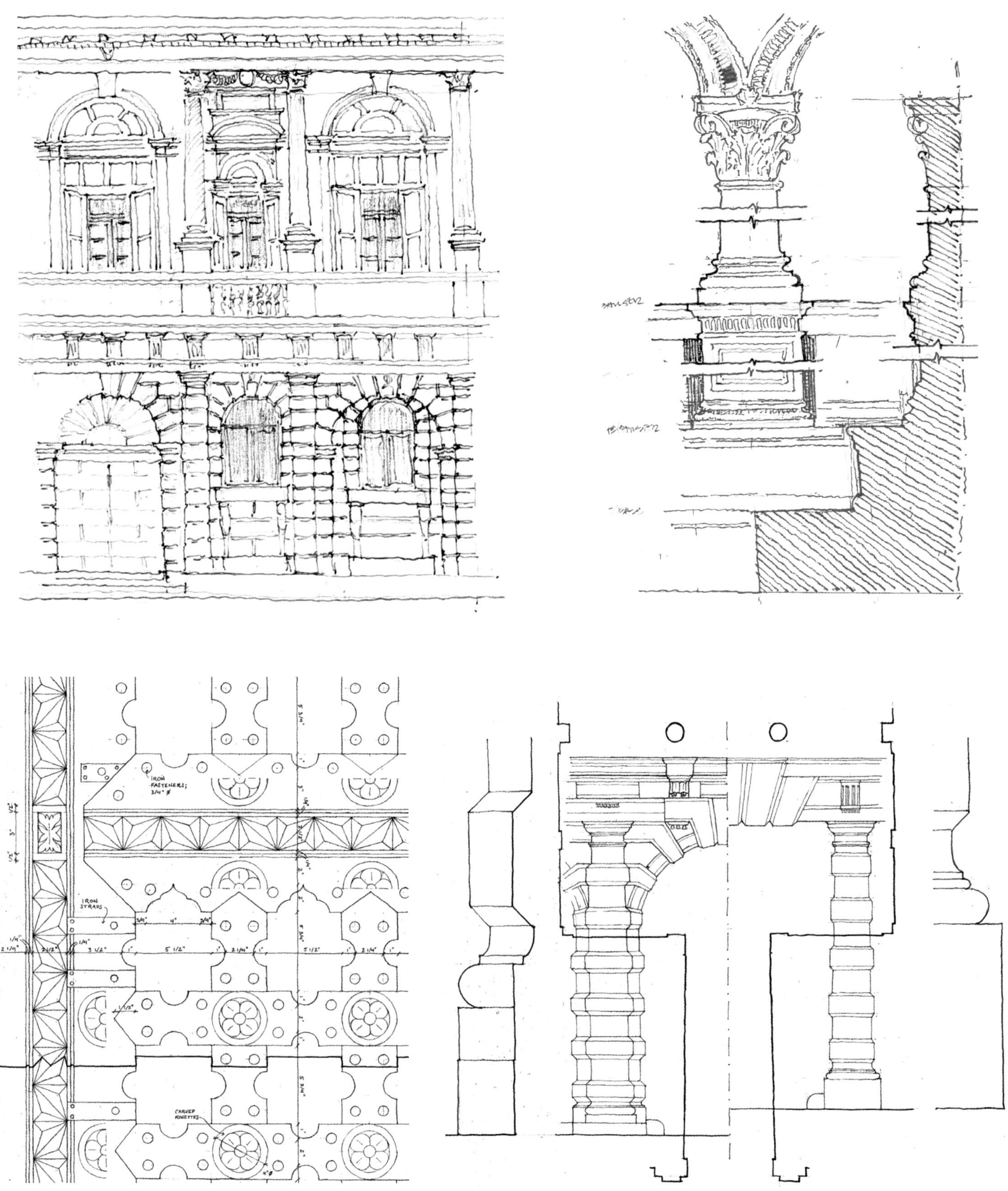

Christopher H. Browne Verona Drawing Tour
(TOP LEFT TO RIGHT) **Palazzo Bevilacqua** and **Loggia del Consiglio,** Christopher Sylva; (BOTTOM LEFT TO RIGHT) **Basilica di Sant'Anastasia** and **Palazzo Maffei,** Taylor Stein; Instructors: Brendan Hart, Meeghan Miller Hart, Michael Mesko

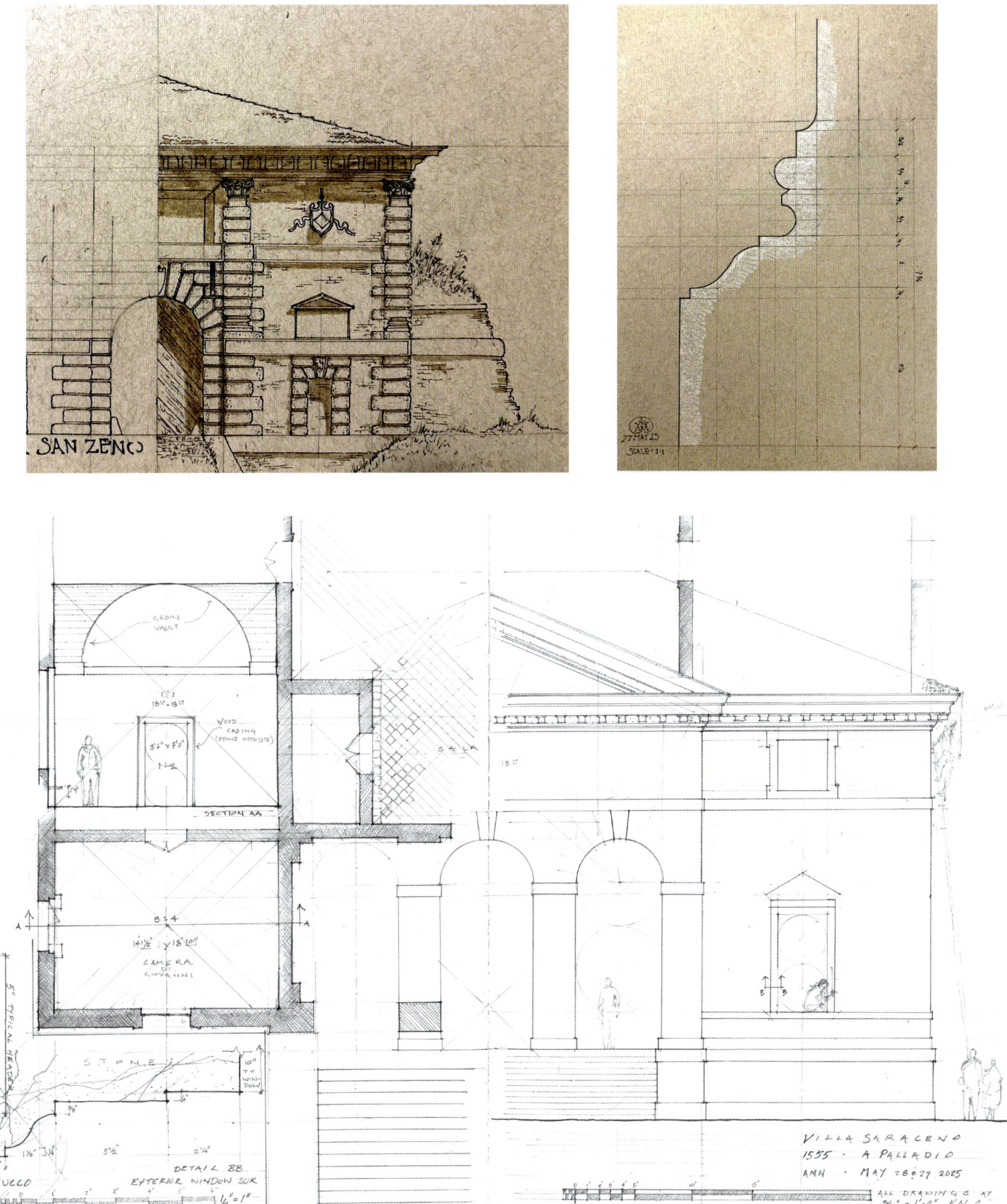

Christopher H. Browne Verona & Villa Saraceno Drawing Tours
(TOP LEFT TO RIGHT) **Porta San Zeno, Verona,** and **Door Entryway, Villa Saraceno,** Jacob Wendt;
(BOTTOM) **Measured Drawing, Villa Saraceno,** Anne Northrop; Instructor: Stephen Chrisman

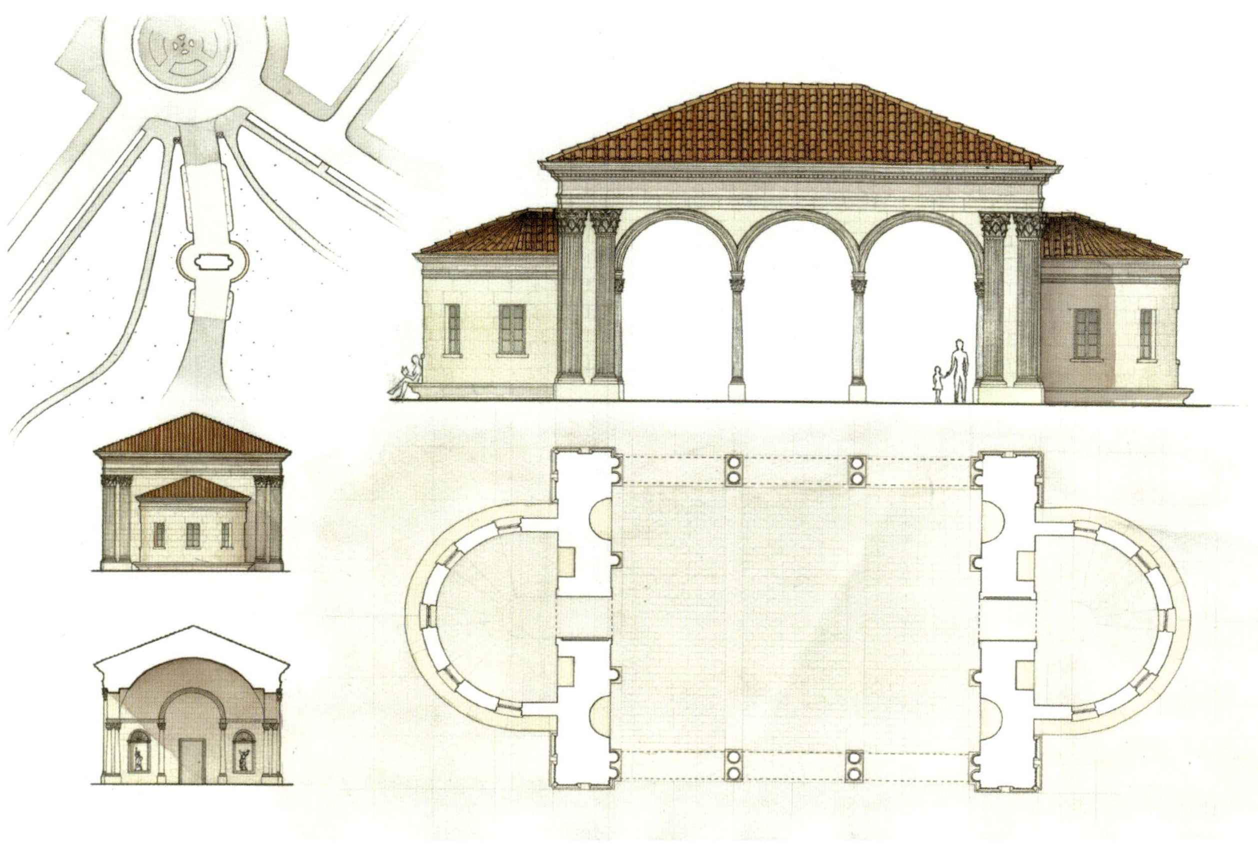

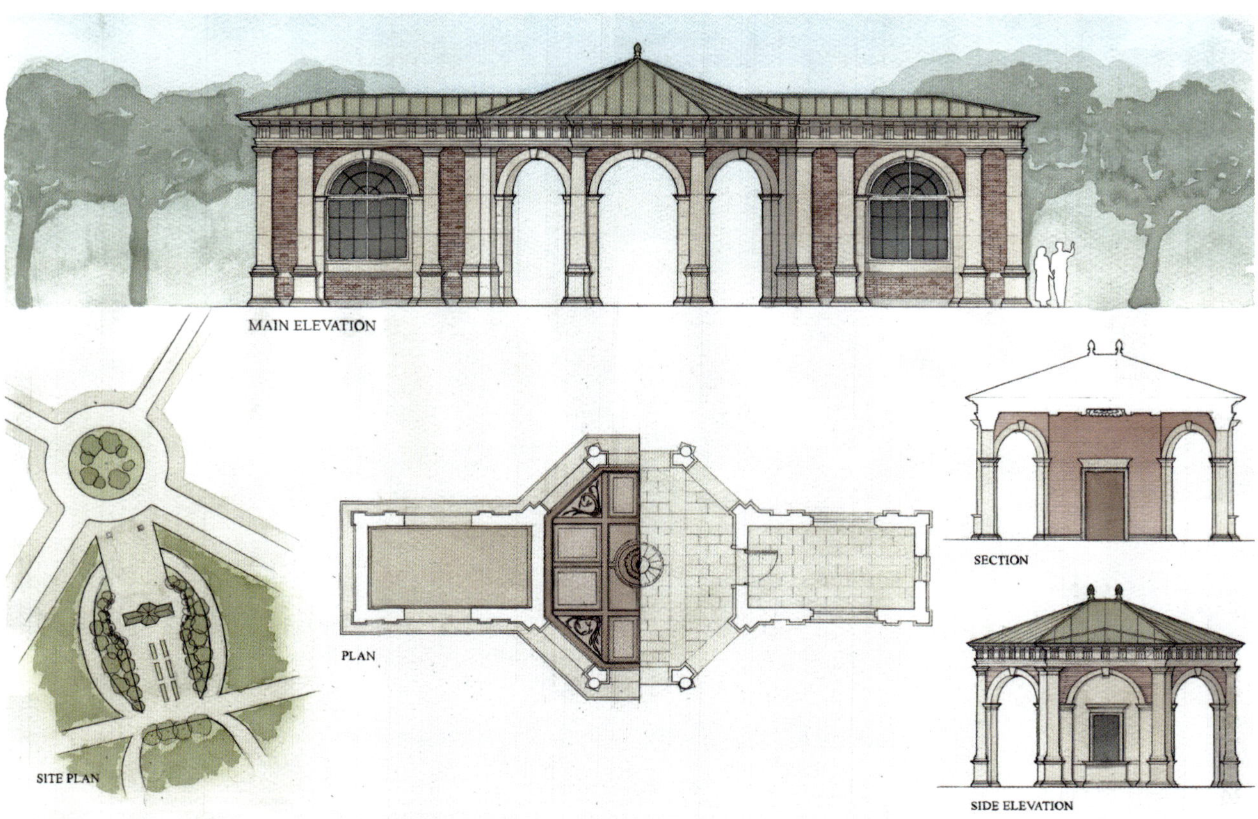

Summer Studio in Classical Architecture, New York City
(TOP TO BOTTOM) **Pavilion in Prospect Park:** Abigail Serban, Stella Xu; Instructors: Keaton Bloom, Jack Edwards, Meeghan Miller Hart, Michael Mesko, Mark Santrach, Charles Shafer, Taylor Stein

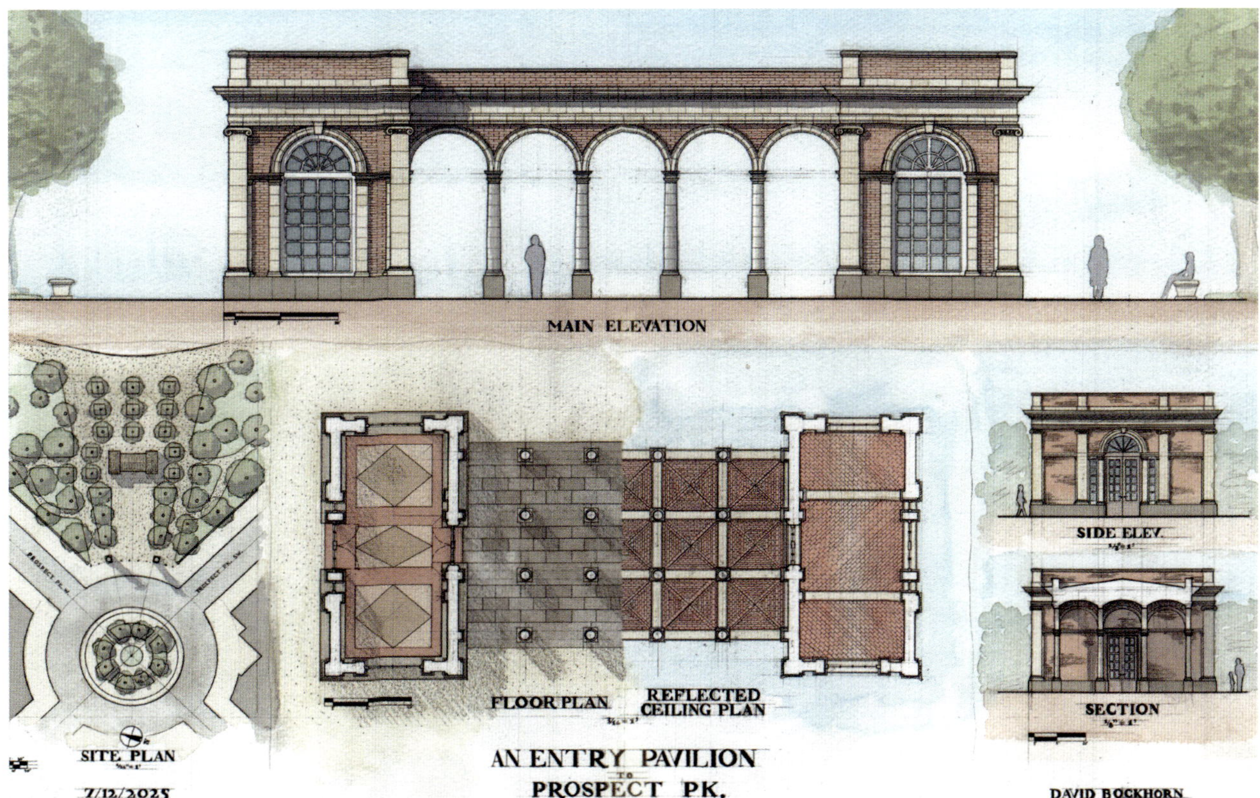

Summer Studio in Classical Architecture, New York City
(TOP TO BOTTOM) **Pavilion in Prospect Park:** Isaiah Kepner, David Bockhorn; Instructors: Keaton Bloom, Jack Edwards, Meeghan Miller Hart, Michael Mesko, Mark Santrach, Charles Shafer, Taylor Stein

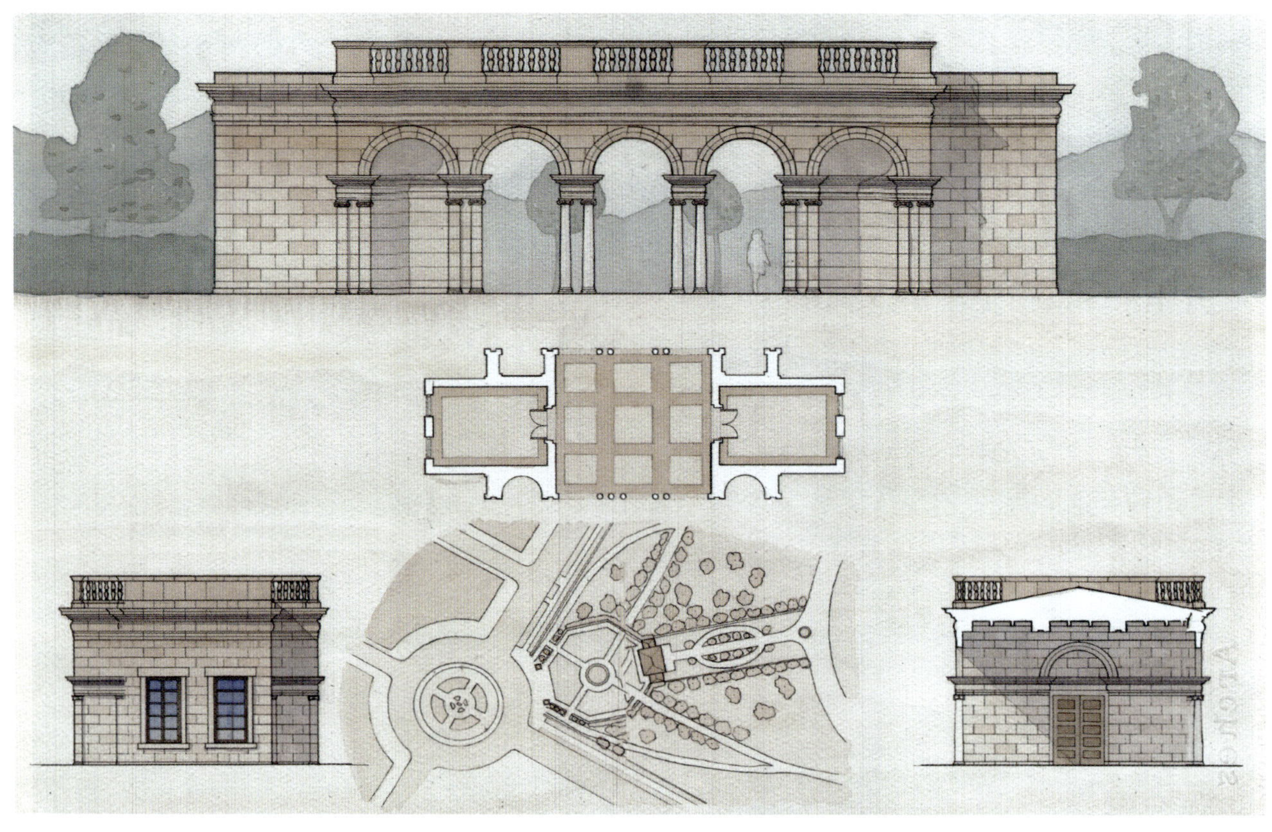

Summer Studio in Classical Architecture, New York City
(TOP TO BOTTOM) **Pavilion in Prospect Park:** Ruth Smedley, Katja Turella; Instructors: Keaton Bloom, Jack Edwards, Meeghan Miller Hart, Michael Mesko, Mark Santrach, Charles Shafer, Taylor Stein

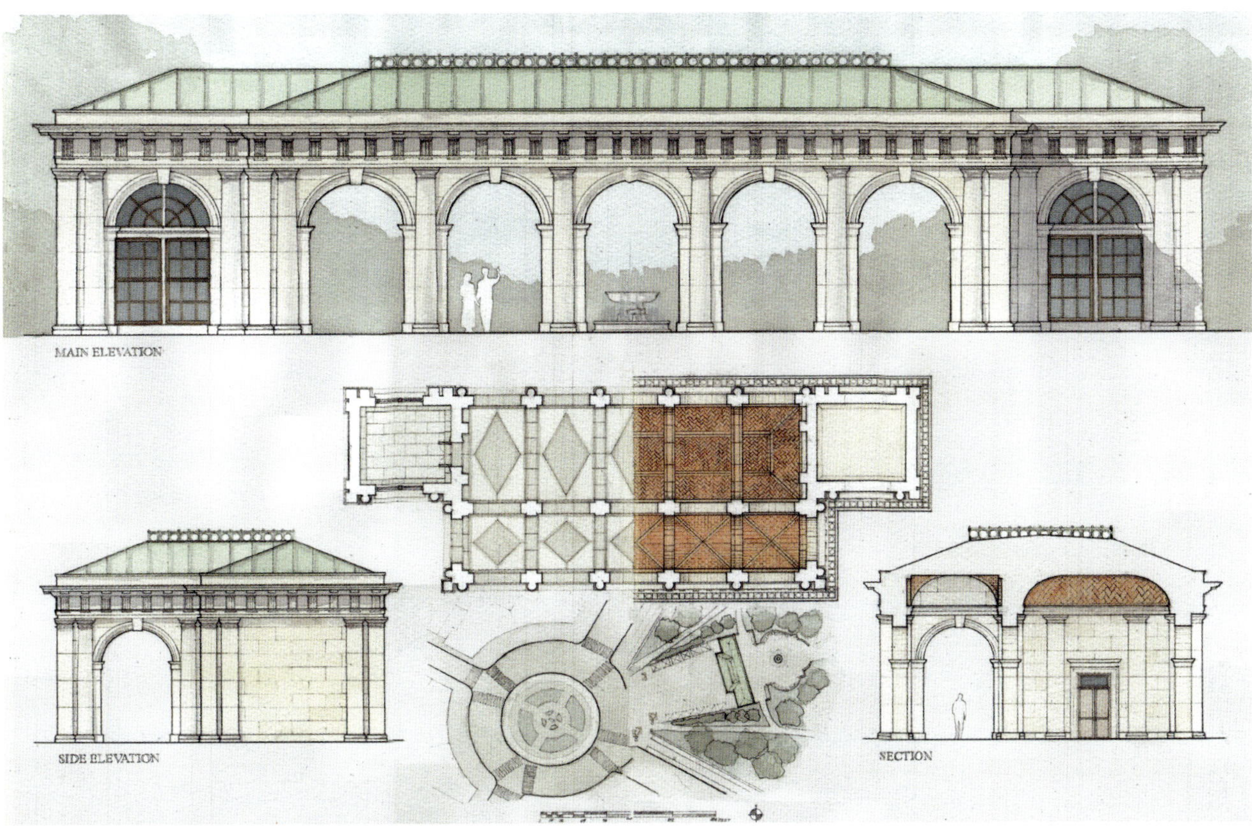

Summer Studio in Classical Architecture, New York City
(TOP TO BOTTOM) **Pavilion in Prospect Park:** Layla Neira, Kathryn Kammerer; Instructors: Keaton Bloom, Jack Edwards, Meeghan Miller Hart, Michael Mesko, Mark Santrach, Charles Shafer, Taylor Stein

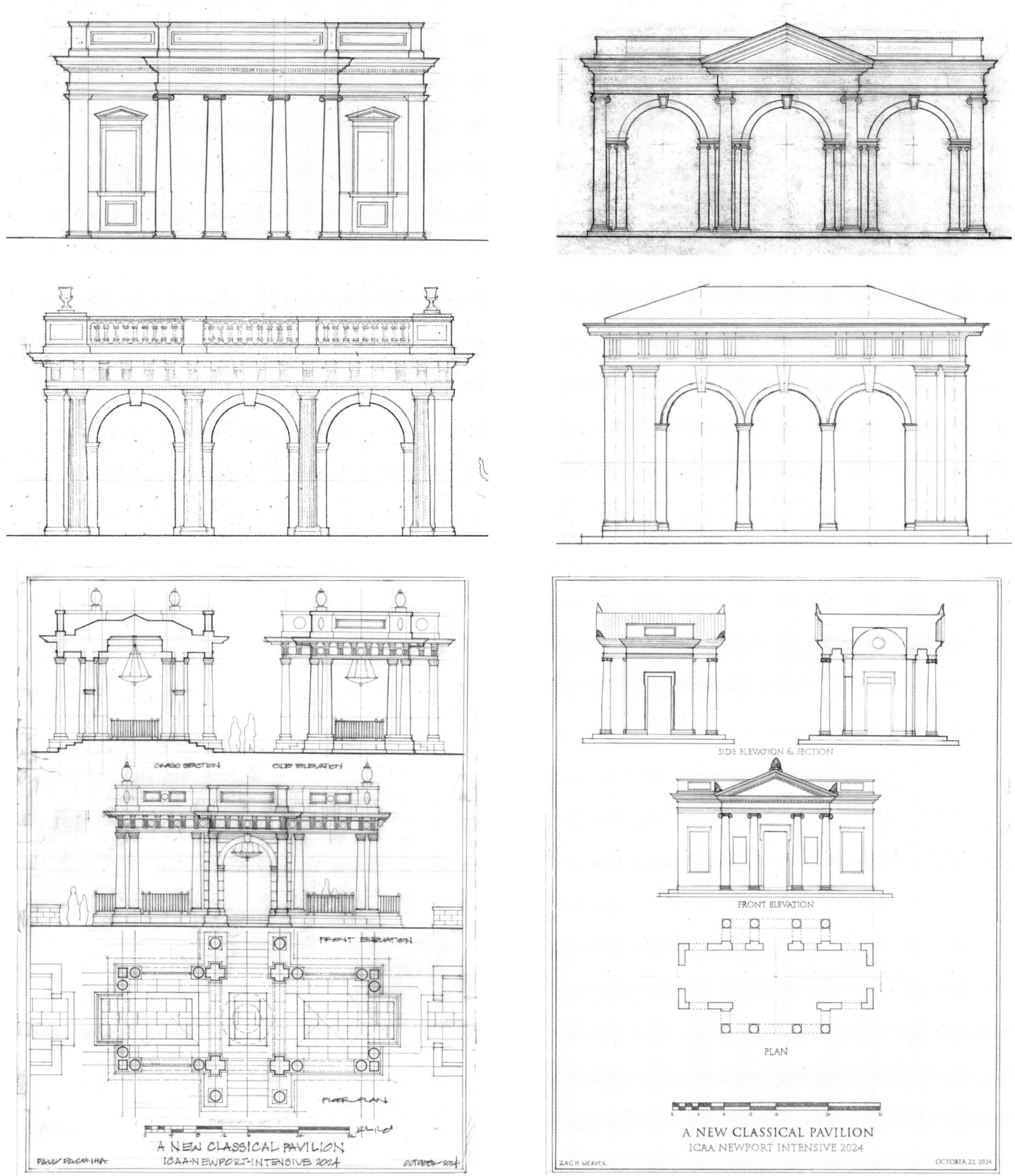

Intensives in Classical Architecture: Newport & New York
(CLOCKWISE FROM TOP LEFT) **New Classical Pavilion, Newport:** Zac Kornis, John Culmone, Joyeux Noel, Zach Weaver, Paul DaCunha; Instructors: Mark Jackson, Michael Mesko, Charles Shafer. **New Classical Pavilion, New York**: Meng Jiang; Instructors: Chris Eiland, Mark Santrach, Nathan Thomas

IBERIAN TRADITIONAL ARCHITECTURE SUMMER SCHOOL

Peneda, Portugal

Project for the Future of Peneda, Peneda, Arcos de Valdevez, Portugal
Summer School Participants' Collaboration; Instructors: José Franqueira Baganha, Fernando Manuel Cerqueira Barros, Aritz Díez Oronoz, Alejandro García Hermida, Imanol Iparraguirre Barbero, Frank Martinez, Lucien Steil

TRADITIONAL ARCHITECTURE GROUP

London, England

(ABOVE CENTER) **Measured Drawing,** Jago Trelawny; (BOTTOM LEFT AND CENTER) **Eastend House, South Lanarkshire** and **Granite Stake Tabernacle, Salt Lake City, Utah,** Ben Felix; (BOTTOM RIGHT) **St. Stephen Walbrook Church, London,** Minty Sainsbury

BENEDICTINE COLLEGE
Atchison, Kansas

Reconstruction of Pliny's Villa, Tuscany, Italy
Peter Sentmanat, 4th Year; Instructor: John Haigh

Reconstruction of Pliny's Villa, Tuscany, Italy
Benjamin Shonka, 4th Year; Instructor: John Haigh

Study of the Ionic Order of the Erechtheion
Emma Howell, 2nd Year; Instructor: Mary Leihy

Lakeside Pavilion Analytique
Benjamin Shonka, 4th Year; Instructor: Jason Baxter

BENEDICTINE COLLEGE

Atchison, Kansas

City Hall for Atchison, Kansas
Peter Zuzolo, 3rd Year; Instructors: Michael Djordjevitch, John Haigh and Ken Heyda

Retreat House, Angel Island, California
Emmett Pauline, 3rd Year; Instructors: John Haigh and Ken Heyda

Estate, Deer Island, New York
Emilie Nelson, 3rd Year; Instructors: John Haigh and Ken Heyda

UNIVERSITY OF COLORADO DENVER

Denver, Colorado

A House of Modest Monumentality, Colorado
Bhudip Gurung, 3rd Year Graduate; Instructor: Laurence Keith Loftin III

YALE UNIVERSITY

New Haven, Connecticut

Gleisdreieck Bridge Temple Market, Berlin, Germany
Megan Ju, 1st Year Graduate; Instructors: Julia Treese and George Knight

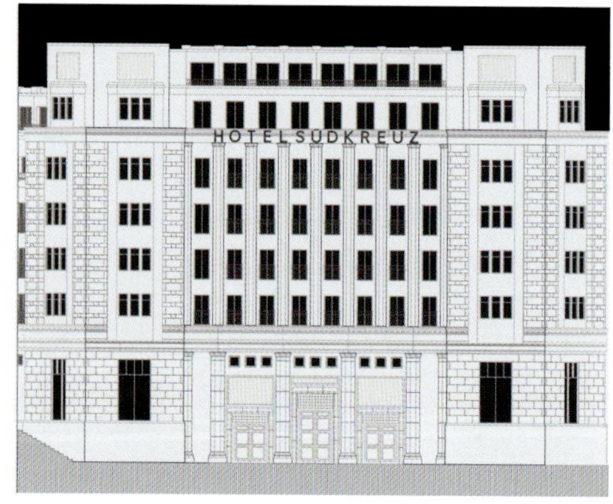

Hotel Südkreuz, Berlin, Germany
Paddy Mittag-McNaught, 3rd Year Graduate; Instructors: Julia Treese and George Knight

AMERICAN COLLEGE OF THE BUILDING ARTS

Charleston, South Carolina

Victorian Botanical Garden and Public Park, Athens, Georgia
Grace Malcolm, 4th Year; Instructor: Jack Duncan

KINGSTON UNIVERSITY

London, England

Market Mews, St Neots, England
Marian Gallagher, 2nd Year Graduate; Instructors: Tom Coward and Bryony Martin

UTAH VALLEY UNIVERSITY

Orem, Utah

Penny Commons, Heber, Utah
Joshua Lythgoe, 5th Year; Instructors: Paul Monson and Jim Nielson

Kai Maluhia (Sea of Peace) Presbyterian Church, Kahuku Point, O'ahu, Hawai'i
Davis McDermott, 4th Year; Instructor: Brandon Ro

Provo 3rd Ward Chapel Analytique, Provo, Utah
Will Newby, 3rd Year; Instructor: Ben Felix

UTAH VALLEY UNIVERSITY

Orem, Utah

National Museum of American Religion, Washington, DC
Will Newby and Nash Rasmussen, 3rd Year; Instructor: Brandon Ro

National Museum of American Religion, Washington, DC
Hunter Ferre and Alexi Fund, 3rd Year; Instructor: Brandon Ro

Temple for The Church of Jesus Christ of Latter-Day Saints, New Cairo, Egypt
Jacob Wendt, 5th Year; Instructors: Paul Monson and Jim Nielson

CATHOLIC UNIVERSITY OF AMERICA
Washington, DC

Old Dominion Pumping Station, Washington, DC
Jackson Hicks, Dylan Robertson, Elizabeth Sypal, 4th Year; Instructors: Timothy Smith and Jonathan Taylor

Institute for Urban Water Ecology, Washington, DC
Sarah Haeflinger and Luke Kelly, 4th Year; Instructors: Timothy Smith and Jonathan Taylor

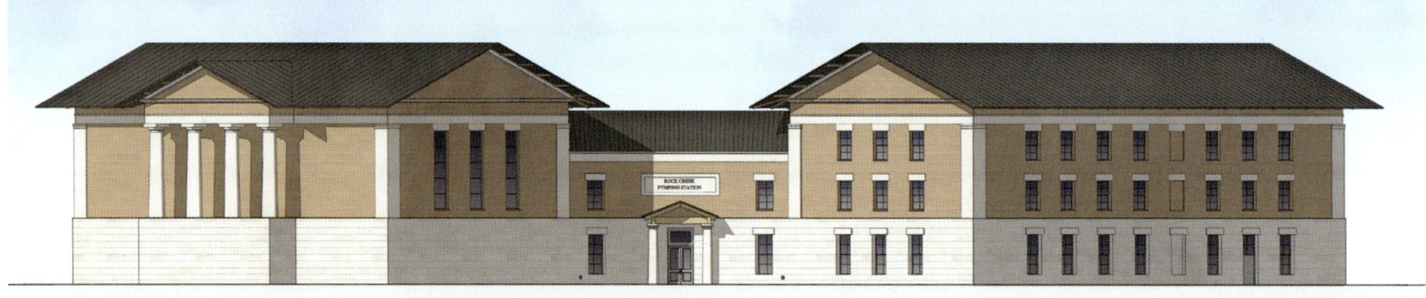

Rock Creek Pumping Station, Washington, DC
Julia Renaghan and Scott Szpisjak, 2nd Year Graduate; Instructors: Timothy Smith and Jonathan Taylor

CATHOLIC UNIVERSITY OF AMERICA

Washington, DC

Oratory for Venerable Father Emil Kapaun, Pilsen, Kansas
Grace Hausladen, 2nd Year Graduate;
Instructor: Christopher J. Howard

Koutoubia Mosque Minaret, Marrakech, Morocco
Ana Schluth, 4th Year;
Instructor: Christopher J. Howard

A People-Centered, Climate-Resilient New Orleans, Lower 9th Ward, New Orleans, Louisiana
Sanaa Dukes, 1st Year Graduate; Instructor: Christopher J. Howard

CATHOLIC UNIVERSITY OF AMERICA
Washington, DC

National Shrine Cathedral of the Holy Family, Kansas City, Kansas
Luke Seymour, 2nd Year Graduate; Instructor: Christopher J. Howard

UNIVERSITY OF NOTRE DAME
Notre Dame, Indiana

Proposal for a New Classics, Humanities, and Linguistics High School
Odessa Weir, 3rd Year; Instructor: Ettore Mazzola

Proposal for a New Classics, Humanities, and Linguistics High School
Christina Janowicz, 3rd Year; Instructor: Ettore Mazzola

UNIVERSITY OF NOTRE DAME

Notre Dame, Indiana

Charlotte Gateway Memorial Station, Charlotte, North Carolina
Peter Galmish, 2nd Year Graduate; Instructor: Lucien Steil

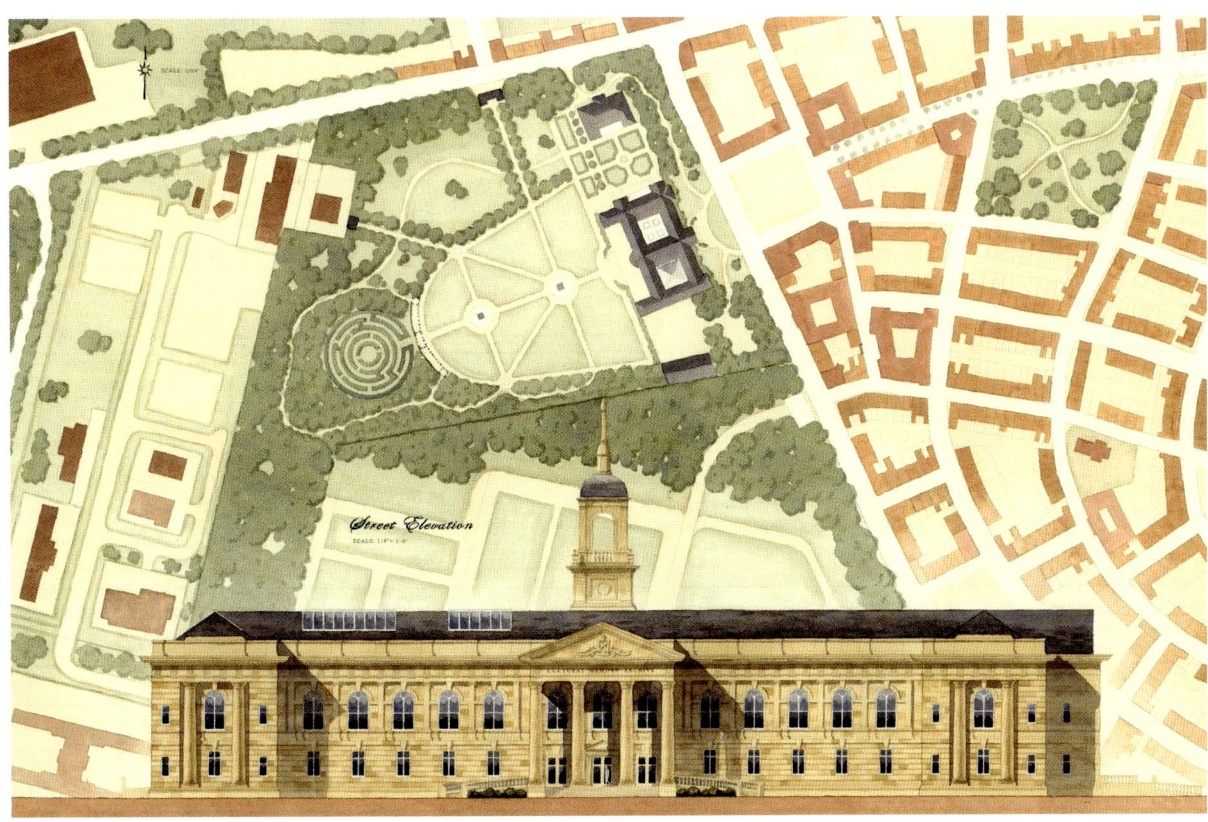

A Cultural Memory Archive, Halftown, Northern Ireland
Erin Panker, 5th Year Thesis; Instructor: Christopher Miller

UNIVERSITY OF NOTRE DAME

Notre Dame, Indiana

Center for the Arts, South Bend, Indiana
Nolan Waters, 2nd Year; Instructors: Andrea Avelar, Meeghan Miller Hart, Brendan Hart, Michael Mesko

Research Library and Archive, Paris, France
Sam Buchanan, 2nd Year; Instructors: Michael Mesko, Sara Bega, Andrea Avelar, Alessandro Pierattini

Research Library and Archive, Paris, France
Henry Djuric, 2nd Year; Instructors: Michael Mesko, Sara Bega, Andrea Avelar, Alessandro Pierattini

A New Town House, Bath, England
(LEFT TO RIGHT) Henry Djuric, Nolan Waters, Matthew Fagerheim, Michael Redfern, 2nd Year; Instructors: Michael Mesko, Sara Bega, Andrea Avelar, Alessandro Pierattini

NOTABLE PRECEDENTS AND BIBLIOGRAPHY

NOTABLE PRECEDENTS

SOUTHWEST OHIO

CINCINNATI

Taft Museum of Art (Baum-Taft House)
Martin Baum, 1820

William Howard Taft House
Built 1840–51

Carew Tower and Netherland Plaza Hotel
Walter W. Ahlschlager and Delano & Aldrich, 1929–30

Old St. Mary's Church
Franz Ignatz Erd, 1841

Cathedral Basilica of St. Peter In Chains
Henry Walter, 1841–45

Spring Grove Cemetery
Howard Daniels & Adolph Strauch, 1844

Cincinnati Observatory
Samuel Hannaford, 1873

Cincinnati Observatory

Cincinnati Music Hall
Samuel Hannaford, 1878

Walnut Hills Branch, Cincinnati Public Library
McLaughlin & Gilmore, 1906

Laurel Court (Peter G. Thomson House)
James Gamble Rogers, 1902–07

Union Central Life Insurance Company (PNC) Building

Cincinnati Art Museum
James W. McLaughlin, Daniel Burnham, Garber & Woodward, 1886–1907

Cincinnati City Hall
Samuel Hannaford, 1893

Gwynne Building
Ernest Flagg, 1913

Union Central Life Insurance Company (PNC Building)
Cass Gilbert, 1913

Western & Southern Life Insurance Company Building
Hake & Kuck, 1916

East Side High School (Withrow University High School)
Frederick Garber, 1919

Cincinnati Gas & Electric Building (Duke Energy Building)
Garber & Woodward with John Russell Pope, 1929

Union Terminal (Cincinnati Museum Center)
Alfred T. Fellheimer, Steward Wagner, and Paul Philippe Cret, 1927–33

Walnut Hills High School
Frederick Garber, 1931

Mount Echo Park Pavilion
R. Carl Freund, 1940

DAYTON

Old Montgomery County Courthouse
Howard Daniels, 1847

Dr. Jefferson A. Walters House
Built 1832; modified 1857

Hawthorn Hill
Schenk & Williams, 1912–14

Old Post Office
James Knox Taylor, 1915

Dayton Daily News Building
Albert Pretzinger, 1908–10

St. Joseph Church
Maginnis & Walsh, 1908–11

Dayton Masonic Center (Dayton Masonic Temple)
Herman & Brown, 1925–28

Dayton Daily News Building

Dayton Art Institute
Edward Brodhead Green, 1930

SPRINGBORO

Null House
Christian & Charles Null, 1798

From left to right: Cincinnati Observatory: James Guilford | Union Central Life Insurance Company (PNC) Building: EEJCC, CC BY-SA 4.0 | Dayton Daily News Building: R. Scott James/Alamy Stock Photo

18TH TO 20TH CENTURY

LEBANON

The Golden Lamb
Ichabod Corwin, 1815

HILLSBORO

Highland County Courthouse
Pleasant Arthur, 1832–34

OXFORD

Lewis Place (President's House), Miami University,
Romeo Lewis, 1839

YELLOW SPRINGS

Antioch Hall, Antioch College,
Alpheus Marshall Merrifield, 1853

EATON

Preble County Courthouse, Harvey H. Hiestand, 1917–18

CENTRAL OHIO

COLUMBUS

Ohio Statehouse
Isaiah Rogers, Nathan B. Kelley, and others, 1861

Franklin Conservatory
J. M. Freese, 1895

Antioch Hall, Antioch College

Columbus Public Library
Albert Randolf Ross, 1907

Ohio National Bank Building
Richards, McCarty & Bulford, 1911

William Oxley Thompson Memorial Library, Ohio State University
Allen & Collens, 1912

LeVeque Tower
C. Howard Crane, 1923–27

Ohio State Office Building (Ohio Judicial Center)
Harry Hake, 1930–33

Columbus Museum of Art
Richards, McCarty & Bulford, 1931

Columbus Public Library

CHILLICOTHE

Adena, Thomas Worthington Estate
Benjamin Latrobe, 1807

61 South Paint Street
Built 1816

62 South Paint Street
Built 1830

Canal Warehouse
Built c. 1830

Atwood-Wilson House
Built by Jacob S. Atwood, 1845

Bartlett-Cunningham-Gerber House
Built 1855

Rosse Hall, Kenyon College

Ross County Courthouse
Collins & Autenrieth, 1855–58

GAMBIER

Rosse Hall, Kenyon College
Charles Romanoff Prezriminsky, 1829

Old Bexley Hall, Kenyon College
Henry Roberts, 1839–43

GRANVILLE

Buxton Inn
Built 1812

St Luke's Episcopal Church
Benjamin Morgan, 1837

Avery-Downer House (Robbins Hunter Museum)
Benjamin Morgan, 1842

Swasey Chapel, Denison University
Arnold Brunner, 1924

MOUNT VERNON

Knox County Courthouse
Daniel Clark, 1854–56

ZANESVILLE

Stone Academy
Built 1809

Old Post Office and Federal Building
George F. Hammond, 1904

NOTABLE PRECEDENTS

Zoar Meeting House

ZOAR

Bimeler Cabin
Joseph Bimeler, 1817

Garden House of Simon Beuter, Historic Zoar Village
Built 1850

Zoar Meeting House
Joseph Bimeler, 1853

CIRCLEVILLE

Renick-Young House (Mount Oval)
Built 1832

PORTSMOUTH

First Presbyterian Church
William Newman, 1849

RICHLAND COUNTY

Malabar Farm
Louis Lamoreux, 1941–45

NORTHWEST OHIO

TOLEDO

Old Post Office
James Knox Taylor, 1911

Toledo Museum of Art
Edward Brodhead Green, 1912; expanded 1933

Northern National Bank
George Mills, 1916

Ashley U.S. Courthouse
Graham H. Woolfall, 1930–33

Peristyle Theater
Edward Brodhead Green, 1933

Toledo Public Library
Hahn & Hayes, 1940

WATERVILLE

Columbian House
John Pray, 1837

FREMONT

Sandusky County Courthouse, Cyrus Williams, 1840–44, 1930

MILAN

Edison Birthplace
Samuel Edison, 1841

OTTAWA

Oliver House
Isaiah Rogers, 1859

Malabar Farm

SOUTH BASS ISLAND

Perry's Victory & International Peace Memorial
Joseph H. Freedlander and Alexander D. Seymour Jr., 1915

KENTON

Hardin County Courthouse
Richards, McCarty & Bulford, 1915

Perry's Victory & International Peace Memorial

NORTHEAST OHIO

CLEVELAND

Hilliard Building
Built 1849–50

Old Stone Church (First Presbyterian Church)
Heard & Porter, 1855

Wade Chapel
Hubbell & Benes, 1893

St. Theodosius Orthodox Cathedral
Frederick C. Baird, 1896

Union Club
Charles Schweinfurth, 1905

Cleveland Trust Company Building
George B. Post; sculptor, Karl Bitter, 1907–8

Trinity Episcopal Cathedral
Charles Schweinfurth, 1907

From left to right: Zoar Meeting House: J. J. Prats, via Historical Marker Database| Malabar Farm: Daniel Borzynski/Alamy Stock Photo | Perry's Victory & International Peace Memorial: The Ohio Collection/Alamy Stock Photo

18TH TO 20TH CENTURY

Federal Building and U.S. Post Office (Howard M. Metzenbaum U.S. Courthouse)
Arnold Brunner, 1908

Carnegie West Branch, Cleveland Public Library
Edward L. Tilton, 1908–10

Cuyahoga County Courthouse
Lehman & Schmitt, 1912

Statler Hotel
George B. Post & Sons, 1912

West Side Market
Hubbell & Benes, 1912

St. Colman Church
Edwin J. Schneider, 1914–18

Guardian Trust Company Building
Walker & Weeks, 1915

Cleveland City Hall
Milton Dyer, 1916

Cleveland Museum of Art
Hubbell & Benes, 1916

Federal Reserve Bank of Cleveland
Walker & Weeks, 1921–23

Cuyahoga County Courthouse

Cleveland City Hall

Union Trust Building
Graham, Anderson, Probst & White, 1922–24

Maltz Performing Arts Center (built as Temple Tifereth-Israel)
Charles Greco, 1924

Cleveland Public Auditorium
J. Harold McDowell and Frederic H. Betz with Frank Walker, 1922–28

Cleveland Public Library
Walker & Weeks, 1925

Fine Arts Garden
Olmsted Brothers, with landscape architects Edward Whiting and Leon Zach, 1925–28

Case Western Reserve University Allen Memorial Medical Library
Walker & Weeks, 1926

Terminal Tower
Graham, Anderson, Probst & White, 1927

St. Luke's Hospital
Hubbell & Benes,1927

Shaker Square
Small & Rowley, 1929

Severance Hall
Walker & Weeks, 1931

JEFFERSON

Giddings Law Office
Leon Ransom Jr., 1823

VALLEY VIEW

Frazee House
Built 1826

GATES MILLS

St. Christopher's-by-the River,
Frank R. Walker and L. G. Rogers, 1853

BRATENAHL

Gwinn
Charles Platt with Warren Manning, 1908

West Side Market

From left to right: Cuyahoga County Courthouse: Joe Hendrickson/Alamy Stock Photo | Cleveland City Hall: Glenn Nagel/Alamy Stock Photo | West Side Market: Philip Scalia/Alamy Stock Photo

NOTABLE PRECEDENTS

Wickliffe City Hall (Coulby)

WICKLIFFE

Wickliffe City Hall (Coulby)
Frederic Striebinger, 1911–13

CLEVELAND HEIGHTS

Tremaine-Gallagher House
Frederic Striebinger, 1914

SHAKER HEIGHTS

Woodbury Elementary School
Charles W. Bates, 1918

PEPPER PIKE

The Country Club
Philip L. Small, 1930

OBERLIN

First Church
Richard Bond, 1842

Oberlin College
Finney Chapel
Cass Gilbert, 1908

Allen Memorial Art Museum
Cass Gilbert, 1917

PAINESVILLE

Rider's Inn
Joseph Rider, 1812

Mathews House
Jonathan Goldsmith, 1829

Painesville City Hall
Jonathan Goldsmith, 1840

Lake County Courthouse
Milton Dyer, 1909–10

AKRON

Hale Farm & Village
Fritch Log Cabin, built 1805

Hale Farmhouse, built 1825–27

Jonathan Goldsmith House (Peck-Robinson House); originally built in Willoughby, Ohio, 1830–32

Stow House, originally built in Stow, Ohio, 1852

Colonel Simon Perkins Mansion
Isaac Ladd, 1835–37

Glendale Cemetery
Albert Sargent, 1839

Stan Hywet Hall and Gardens
F. A. Seiberling, 1911; Warren Manning, 1912–15

HUDSON

Baldwin Buss House
Lemuel Porter, 1825

Mathews House

Western Reserve Academy
Lemuel and Simeon Porter, J.W.C. Corbusier, 1829–1922

Western Reserve Academy Chapel
Simeon and Lemuel Porter, 1836

Hayden Hall
Built 1879; remodeled by J. W. Ellsworth, 1908

Jonathan Goldsmith House, Hale Farm

NILES

McKinley Memorial Library
McKim Mead & White, 1817

KINSMAN

Peter Allen House
Willis Smith, 1821

TALLMADGE

Tallmadge Church
Lemuel Porter, 1825

CLARIDON

First Congregational Church
John Talbot and Rufus Hurlburt, 1831

From left to right: Wickliffe City Hall (Coulby): Tim Evanson, CC BY-SA 2.0 | Mathews House: via Ohio History Connection | Jonathan Goldsmith House, Hale Farm: Courtesy of David Ellison

18TH TO 20TH CENTURY

Kingwood

WARREN

Kinsman House
Isaac Ladd, 1832

Warren G. Harding High School
Van Leyen, Schilling & Keogh, 1925

MANSFIELD

Kingwood
Clarence Mack; Pitkin & Mott (gardens), 1926

SANDUSKY

Follett House Museum
Oran Follett, 1834–37

303 East Washington St
Sheldon Smith, 1848

TWINSBURG

1st Congregational Church
Simeon Porter, 1848

UNIONVILLE

Unionville Tavern
Built 1798

Shandy Hall
Built 1815–35

VERMILION

Ritter Public Library
George Ritter, 1958

Kirtland Temple, Kirtland
Joseph Smith, 1836

BURTON

Cook House
Built 1806

Boughton House
Built 1834

YOUNGSTOWN

Mahoning County Courthouse
Charles F. Owsley, 1908–10

Butler Institute of American Art
McKim, Mead & White, 1919

John Rankin House

Stambaugh Auditorium
Harvey Wiley Corbett, 1926

CANTON

Stark County Courthouse
George F. Hammond, 1895

SOUTHEAST OHIO

ATHENS

Cutler Hall, Ohio University,
Benjamin Corp, 1816

Old Post Office
William W. Cooke, 1906

MARIETTA

Erwin Hall
Rufus Erastus Hart, 1850

Washington County Courthouse
Samuel Hannaford & Sons, 1901–2

GALLIPOLIS

Our House Tavern
Built 1819

RIPLEY

John Rankin House
Built 1828

SOMERSET

Perry County Courthouse
(Somerset Village Hall)
Plans by James Hampson, Esq., built 1829–29

POMEROY

Meigs County Courthouse
S. S. Bergin, 1845–48

GEORGETOWN

Brown County Courthouse
Hubbard Baker, 1849

Butler Institute of American Art

From left to right: Kingwood: The Jacksons Photography/Kingwood Center Gardens | John Rankin House: via ohiotraveler.com | Butler Institute of American Art: Randy Duchaine /Alamy Stock Photo

SELECTED BIBLIOGRAPHY

ON OHIO ARCHITECTURE

Allen, Richard Sanders. *Covered Bridges of the Middle West: Ohio, Minnesota, Michigan, Illinois, Wisconsin, Iowa, Indiana, Missouri, Kansas.* Brattleboro, VT: Stephen Greene Press, 1970.

Allyn, Elizabeth P., Elisabeth H. Tuttle, and Katharine F. Willi. *A Guide to Historic Houses in Ohio Open to the Public.* Cincinnati, OH: National Society of the Colonial Dames of America in the State of Ohio, 1996.

Armstrong, Foster, Richard Klein, and Cara Armstrong. *A Guide to Cleveland's Sacred Landmarks.* Kent, OH: Kent State University Press, 1992.

Barrow, William C. "The Mall." *Encyclopedia of Cleveland History,* https://case.edu/ech/articles/m/mall.

Berkhofer, George H. *No Place Like Home: A History of the Domestic Architecture in Springfield and Clark County, Ohio.* Wilmington, OH: Orange Frazer Press, 2007.

Betti, Tom, and Doreen Uhas Sauer. *Forgotten Landmarks of Columbus.* Charleston, SC: The History Press, 2021.

Brunner, Arnold. "Cleveland's Group Plan." *Proceedings of the Eighth National Conference on City Planning, Cleveland, June 5–7, 1916.* New York: National Conference on City Planning, 1916: 14–34. https://wayback.archive-it.org/2566/20211028212129/http://urbanplanning.library.cornell.edu/DOCS/brunner.htm.

Campen, Richard N. *Architecture of the Western Reserve, 1800–1900.* Kent, OH: Kent State University Press, 1971.

Campen, Richard N. *Distinguished Homes of Shaker Heights: An Architectural Overview.* Fort Myers, FL: West Summit Press, 1992.

Campen, Richard N. *Ohio: An Architectural Portrait.* Fort Myers, FL: West Summit Press, 1973.

Campen, Richard N. *Outdoor Sculpture in Ohio.* Fort Myers, FL: West Summit Press, 1980.

Centner, Randy, and Philip Farr. *Cincinnati Sculpture Unveiled: The Story Behind the Art.* Milford, OH: Little Miami Publishing, 2006.

Cigliano, Jan. *Showplace of America: Cleveland's Euclid Avenue, 1850–1910.* Kent, OH: Kent State University Press, 1991.

Cigliano, Jan, and Sarah Bradford Landau, eds. *The Grand American Avenue, 1850–1920.* San Francisco: Pomegranate Artbooks, 1994.

Clubbe, John. Cincinnati *Observed: Architecture and History.* Columbus, OH: Ohio State University Press, 1992.

Comer, Lee, and Ted Ligibel. *Lights Along the River: Landmark Architecture of the Maumee River Valley.* Maumee, OH: Landmarks Committee of the Maumee Valley Historical Society, 1983.

CSU Center for Public History and Digital Humanities. "University Circle," *Cleveland Historical,* https://clevelandhistorical.org/items/show/30.

Cummings, Abbott Lowell. *The Alfred Kelley House of Columbus, Ohio: The Home of a Pioneer Statesman.* Columbus, OH: Franklin County Historical Society, 1953.

DeMarco, Laura. *Cleveland Then and Now.* London: Pavilion Books, 2018.

DeMarco, Laura. *Lost Cleveland.* London: Pavilion Books, 2017.

Dorsey, Robert W., ed. *Architecture and Construction in Cincinnati, Volume I: A Guide to Buildings Designers and Builders.* Cincinnati, OH: Architectural Foundation of Cincinnati, 1987.

Drinkle, Ruth Wolfley. *Heritage of Architecture and Arts: Fairfield County, Ohio.* Lancaster, OH: Fairfield Heritage Association, 1978.

Ellis, Anita, and Walter Langsam. *An Expression of the Community: Cincinnati Public Schools Legacy of Art and Architecture.* Cincinnati, OH: Art League Press, 2014.

Ellis Jr., Lloyd R. *A Guide to Greater Cleveland's Sacred Landmarks.* Kent, OH: Kent State University Press, 2012.

Evans, Bruce H. *Fifty Treasures of the Dayton Art Institute.* Dayton, OH: Dayton Art Institute, 1970.

Fanning, Kay, and Thomas E. Luebke. *American Shrines: The Architecture of Presidential Commemoration.* Amherst: University of Massachusetts Press, 2025.

Fazio, Michael, and Patrick Snadon. *The Domestic Architecture of Benjamin Henry Latrobe.* Baltimore: Johns Hopkins University Press, 2005.

The Federal Writers' Project. *The Ohio Guide* (American Guide Series). Washington, DC: Works Progress Administration, 1940.

The Federal Writers' Project. *Cincinnati: A Guide to the Queen City and Its Neighbors.* Washington, DC: Works Progress Administration, 1940.

Frary, I. T. *Early Homes of Ohio.* Richmond, VA: Garrett & Massie, 1936.

Franklin, David. *The CMA Companion: A Guide to the Cleveland Museum of Art.* Cleveland, OH: Cleveland Museum of Art; New York: Scala Arts Publishers, 2014.

Gaede, Robert C. *Guide to Cleveland Architecture.* Cleveland, OH: AIA Cleveland, 1997.

Giglierano, Jeffrey J., and Deborah A. Overmeyr with Frederick I. Propoas. *The Bicentennial Guide to Greater Cincinnati: A Portrait of Two Hundred Years.* Cincinnati, OH: Cincinnati Historical Society, 1988.

Gorczyca, Beth. *Ohio's Bicentennial Barns: A Collection of the Historic Barns Celebrating Ohio's Bicentennial.* Wooster, OH: Wooster Book Company, 2003.

Gormley, D. Michael. *Federal Art in Cleveland, 1933–1943.* Cleveland, OH: Cleveland Public Library, 1974.

Graham, A. A., and S. Colborn, eds. *History of Fairfield and Perry Counties, Ohio.* Chicago: W. Beers & Co., 1883.

Graichen, Jody H. *Remembering German Village: Columbus, Ohio's Historic Treasure.* Charleston, SC: The History Press, 2010.

Hamlin, Talbot. *Greek Revival Architecture in America.* Oxford: Oxford University Press, 1944.

Harwood Jr., Herbert H. *Invisible Giants: The Empires of Cleveland's Van Sweringen Brothers.* Bloomington: Indiana University Press, 2003.

Herrick, Clay. *Cleveland Landmarks.* Cleveland, OH: Cleveland Landmarks Commission, 1996.

Hitchcock, Elizabeth G. *Jonathan Goldsmith: Pioneer Master Builder in the Western Reserve.* Cleveland, OH: Western Reserve Historical Society, 1980.

Hiti, Anthony. *Charles F. Schweinfurth: Uncompromising Architect of Cleveland's Valiant Age.* Cleveland, OH: Artneo, 2013.

Hutslar, Donald A. *Log Construction in the Ohio Country, 1750–1850.* Athens: Ohio University Press, 1992.

Johannesen, Eric. *Cleveland Architecture, 1876–1976.* Cleveland, OH: Western Reserve Historical Society, 1979.

Johannesen, Eric. *A Cleveland Legacy: The Architecture of Walker and Weeks.* Kent, OH: Kent State University Press, 1998.

Johannesen, Eric. *Ohio College Architecture Before 1870.* Columbus: Ohio Historical Society, 1969.

Kapsch, Robert J. *Canals (Library of Congress Visual Sourcebooks).* New York: W. W. Norton & Co., 2004.

Karson, Robin S. *The Muses of Gwinn: Art and Nature in a Garden Designed by Warren H. Manning, Charles A. Platt and Ellen Biddle Shipman.* Sagaponack, NY: Sagapress, 1995.

Katz, Wendy Jean. *Regionalism and Reform: Art and Class Formation in Antebellum Cincinnati.* Columbus, OH: Ohio State University Press, 2002.

Kennedy, Roger G. *Hidden Cities: The Discovery and Loss of Ancient North American Civilization.* New York: Free Press, 1994.

Kidney, Walter C. *Historic Buildings of Ohio.* Pittsburgh, PA: Ober Park Associates, 1972.

Langsam, Walter. *Great Houses of the Queen City: Two Hundred Years of Historic & Contemporary Architecture & Interiors in Cincinnati & Northern Kentucky.* Cincinnati, OH: Cincinnati Historical Society, 1997.

Ledebur, Larry C., and Susan L. Whitelaw. *Village Landmark Churches of Northeast Ohio.* Cleveland, OH: Cleveland State University, 2006.

Leedy, Walter C. *Cleveland Builds an Art Museum: Patronage, Politics, and Architecture, 1884–1916.* Cleveland, OH: Cleveland Museum of Art, 1991.

Love, Jeannine deNobel. *Cleveland Architecture, 1890–1930: Building the City Beautiful.* East Lansing: Michigan State University Press, 2020.

Love, Steve. *Stan Hywet Hall & Gardens.* Akron, OH: University of Akron Press, 2000.

Maxwell, Sidney Denise. *The Suburbs of Cincinnati: Sketches Historical and Descriptive.* Cincinnati, OH: G. E. Stevens & Co., 1870.

McCormick, Virginia E. *Educational Architecture in Ohio: From One-Room Schools and Carnegie Libraries to Community Education Villages.* Kent, OH: Kent State University Press, 2001.

Merkel, Jayne, and Kevin Grace. *The University of Cincinnati Architectural Transformation: Tradition and Innovation.* Cincinnati, OH: RAF Press, 2007.

Miller, Zane L., and Bruce Tucker. *Changing Plans for America's Inner Cities: Cincinnati's Over-the-Rhine and Twentieth Century Urbanism.* Columbus, OH: The Ohio State University Press, 1997.

Miller, Zane L. *Visions of Place: The City, Neighborhoods, Suburbs, and Cincinnati's Clifton, 1850–2000.* Columbus, OH: The Ohio State University Press, 2001.

Moorman, Jane. *Ohio State Capitol, Columbus.* Self-published, 2025.

Newcomb, Rexford. *Architecture of the Old Northwest Territory: A Study of Early Architecture in Ohio, Indiana, Illinois, Michigan, Wisconsin, & Part of Minnesota.* Chicago: University of Chicago Press, 1950.

Newkirk, Lois, ed. *Hudson: A Survey of Historic Buildings in an Ohio Town.* Kent, OH: Kent State University Press, 1989.

Nicoletta, Julie, and Bret Morgan. *The Architecture of the Shakers.* Woodstock: The Countryman Press, 1995.

O'Gorman, James. *Isaiah Rogers: Architectural Practice in Antebellum America.* Boston: University of Massachusetts Press, 2015.

Pacini, Lauren R. *Empire Builders: An Illustrated History of the Rise and Fall of Cleveland's Van Sweringen Brothers.* Bloomington: Indiana University Press, 2024.

Painter, Sue Ann. *Architecture in Cincinnati: An Illustrated History of Designing and Building an American City.* Athens: Ohio University Press, in association with the Architectural Foundation of Cincinnati, 2006.

Parks, Warren Wright. *The Mariemont Story: "A National Exemplar in Town Planning."* Cincinnati, OH: Creative Writers and Publishers, 1967.

Perkins, Michael A. *Leveque: The First Complete Story of Columbus' Greatest Skyscraper.* Bloomington, IN: Author House, 2005.

Phillips, Hazel Spencer. *Traditional Architecture, Warren County, Ohio.* Lebanon, OH: self-published, 1969.

Piña, Leslie A. *Louis Rorimer: A Man of Style.* Kent, OH: Kent State University Press, 1990.

Raponi, Richard, and Michael Rotman. "Group Plan: The New Center That Wasn't," *Cleveland Historical*, https://clevelandhistorical.org/items/show/56.

Rarick, Holly M. *Progressive Vision: The Planning of Downtown Cleveland, 1903–1930.* Cleveland, OH: Cleveland Museum of Art in cooperation with Indiana University Press, 1986.

Reflections: The American Collection of the Columbus Museum of Art. Columbus, OH: Columbus Museum of Art; Athens: Ohio University Press, 2019.

Rogers, Millard F., Jr. *John Nolen & Mariemont: Building a New Town in Ohio.* Baltimore: Johns Hopkins University Press, 2001.

Rose, Linda C., Patrick Rose, and Gibson Yungblut. *Cincinnati Union Terminal: An Art Deco Masterpiece.* Cincinnati, OH Railroad Club, Inc., 1999.

Roy, Christopher. "University Circle," *Encyclopedia of Cleveland History.* https://case.edu/ech/articles/u/university-circle.

Ryberg-Webster, Stephanie. *Preserving the Vanishing City: Historic Preservation amid Urban Decline in Cleveland, Ohio.* Philadelphia: Temple University Press, 2023.

Sauer, Doreen Uhas, and Kathy Mast Kane. *Columbus and the Ohio State University: Then and Now.* San Diego, CA: Thunder Bay Press, 2009.

Schofield, Mary-Peale. "The Cleveland Arcade." *Journal of the Society of Architectural Historians* 25, vol. 4 (1966): 281–91.

Schofield, Mary-Peale. *Landmark Architecture of Cleveland.* Pittsburgh, PA: Ober Park Associates, Inc., 1976.

Schwartz, James. *Hamilton, Ohio: Its Architecture and History.* Hamilton, OH: Hamilton City Planning Department, 1986.

Smith, Ophia D. *Old Oxford Houses and the People Who Lived in Them.* Oxford, OH: Miami University Alumni Association, 1975.

Souther, J. Mark. *Believing in Cleveland: Managing Decline in "the Best Location in the Nation."* Philadelphia: Temple University Press, 2017.

Souther, J. Mark. "Euclid Ave." *Encyclopedia of Cleveland History.* https://case.edu/ech/articles/e/euclid-ave.

Souther, J. Mark. "Public Square." *Cleveland Historical*, https://clevelandhistorical.org/items/show/22.

Stechow, Wolfgang. *Catalogue of European and American Paintings and Sculpture in the Allen Memorial Art Museum, Oberlin College.* Oberlin, OH: Oberlin College, 1967.

Stephenson, R. Bruce. *John Nolen, Landscape Architect and City Planner.* Amherst: University of Massachusetts Press, in association with Library of American Landscape History, 2021.

Stern, Robert A. M., David Fishman, and Jacob Tilove. *Paradise Planned: The Garden Suburb and the Modern City.* New York: The Monacelli Press, 2013.

Straker, Cheryl J. *Ohio Statehouse: A Building for the Ages.* Virginia Beach, VA: Donning Co. Publishers, 2011.

Suess, Jeff. *Lost Cincinnati.* Charleston, SC: The History Press, 2015.

Suess, Jeff. *Cincinnati Then and Now.* London: Pavilion Books, 2018.

Sweetkind, Irene S., ed. *Index to the Permanent Collection: The Butler Institute of American Art.* Youngstown, OH: Butler Institute of American Art, 1997.

Taft Museum of Art. *Taft Museum of Art: An Illustrated Guide.* Lawrenceburg, IN: R. L. Ruehrwein, 2005.

Thrane, Susan W. *County Courthouses of Ohio.* Bloomington: Indiana University Press, 2000.

Toledo Museum of Art. *The Toledo Museum of Art: A Guide to the*

Collections. Toledo, OH: Toledo Museum of Art, 1976.

Toman, James A., and Daniel J. Cook. *Cleveland's Towering Treasure: A Landmark Turns 75.* Cleveland, OH: Cleveland Landmarks Press, 2004.

Toman, James A., and Gregory G. Deegan. *Cleveland Stadium: The Last Chapter, 1931–1996.* Cleveland, OH: Cleveland Landmarks Press, 1997.

Turner, Julie D. *Best-Laid Plans: The Promises and Pitfalls of the New Deal Greenbelt Towns.* Cincinnati, OH: University of Cincinnati Press, 2023.

Vacha, John. *Meet Me on Lake Erie, Dearie!: Cleveland's Great Lakes Exposition, 1936–1937.* Kent, OH: Kent State University Press, 2011.

Van Hook, Bailey. *The Virgin and the Dynamo: Public Murals in American Architecture, 1893–1917.* Athens: Ohio University Press, 2003.

Vitz, Robert C. *The Queen and the Arts: Cultural Life in Nineteenth-Century Cincinnati.* Kent, OH: Kent State University Press, 1989.

Walsh, Andrew. *Lost Dayton, Ohio.* Charleston, SC: The History Press, 2018.

Ware, Jane. *Building Ohio: A Traveler's Guide to Ohio's Urban Architecture, Volume I.* Wilmington, OH: Orange Frazer Press, 2001.

Ware, Jane. *Building Ohio: A Traveler's Guide to Ohio's Urban Architecture, Volume II.* Wilmington, OH: Orange Frazer Press, 2002.

Weiner, Mina Rieur, ed. *Edwin Howland Blashfield: Master American Muralist.* New York: W. W. & Co., 2009.

White, Virginia S. *Treasured Landmarks of Indian Hill.* Cincinnati, OH: Indian Hill Historical Society/Cincinnati Preservation Association, 1993.

Wilson, Richard Guy, and Sidney K. Robinson, eds. *Modern Architecture in America: Visions and Revisions.* Ames: Iowa State University Press, 1991.

Wolf, Michael Allan. *The Zoning of America: Euclid v. Ambler.* Lawrence: University Press of Kansas, 2008.

Ziff, Katherine. *Asylum on the Hill: History of a Healing Landscape.* Athens: Ohio University Press, 2018.

SPONSORS

BELT • METAL ART+DESIGN STUDIO

Brookes & Henderson Building Co.

Carolyn Thayer Interiors

Chadsworth Incorporated

Cooper Historical Windows

D. H. Ellison Co.

Dalgliesh Gilpin Paxton Architects

Dan Gordon Landscape Architects

Debra Antolino Interiors, Inc.

DONADIC

E. F. San Juan, Inc.

E.R. Butler & Co.

Emily Summers Design Associates

Eric J. Smith Architect PC

Ferguson & Shamamian Architects

Flower Construction

Haddonstone

John B. Murray Architect

Kathryn Herman Design

L. Lumpkins Architects, Inc.

Mark P. Finlay Architects, AIA

Michael Simon Interiors, Inc.

Patrick Sutton Interior Design

Peter Zimmerman Architects

RAMSA (Robert A.M. Stern Architects)

SEBASTIAN

Skurman Architects

Steven W Spandle Architect

Vella Interiors Inc.

Winchester

Woolems, Inc.

Zepsa Industries Inc.

WINCHESTER
W
45 YEARS OF FINE BUILDING
winchesterinc.com

E.R. Butler & Co.

Massachusetts Charitable Mechanic Association
Triennial Exhibitions & Fairs

Enoch Robinson & Henry Whitney (1826)

G.W. Robinson & Co. (1832–1873)

Enoch Robinson & Francis Draper (1833–1837)

E. Robinson & Co. (1839–1905)

Wm. Hall & Co. (1843–1919)

G.N. Wood & Co. (1905–1915)

John Tein Company (1883–1939)

L.S. Hall & Co. (1911–1918)

W.C. Vaughan Co. (1902-2000)

Ostrander & Eshleman (1921–1992)

Quincy Spindle Mfg. Co. (–1999)
(New England Lock and Hardware Co.)

Edward R. Butler Company (1966–1990)

&

E.R. Butler & Co. (1990–)

Design for the Massachusetts Charitable Mechanic Association Diploma, Charles Howland Hammatt Billings, 1860
Library of Congress, Prints and Photographs Division

E. Robinson & Co.

BLACK GLASS CABINET KNOB & ROSE

With Blind Mount

US Patent 434, "Method of Attaching Glass Knobs to Metallic Sockets"

1.45 × 1.45 × 2.6 in. (Projection × Width × Overall Length)

J.P. Cushing Estate "Bellmont," 1840

Belmont, Mass.

Asher Benjamin, Architect

E.R. Butler & Co. Research Library Archives

E. Robinson & Co.

SILVERED GLASS DOOR KNOB & ROSE

With Blind Mount

US Patent 434, "Method of Attaching Glass Knobs to Metallic Sockets"

1.75 × 1.75 × 3.5 in. (Projection × Width × Overall Length)

Catherine Hammond Gibson House, 1860

Boston, Mass.

Edward Clarke Cabot, Architect

E.R. Butler & Co. Research Library Archives

MASSACHUSETTS CHARITABLE MECHANIC ASSOCIATION
ENOCH ROBINSON, SILVER MEDALS, 1841 & 1881

Awarded at the Third Triennial Exhibition of the MCMA, September 20, 1841
Awarded at the Fourteenth Triennial Exhibition of the MCMA, September 13, 1881

Engraved by Christian Gobrecht (Top Row)
Engraved by Francis Napoleon Mitchell (Bottom Row)
E.R. Butler & Co. Research Library Archives

MASSACHUSETTS CHARITABLE MECHANIC ASSOCIATION

Triennial Exhibitions & Fairs

"For the Encouragement of Manufactures and the Mechanic Arts"

SELECTED REPORTS OF THE JUDGES

1841 (SEPTEMBER 20), Third Triennial Exhibition of the Massachusetts Charitable Mechanic Association. Boston.

The committee commenced the work assigned them, by first examining articles entered under Nos. 877, 558, and 623; and they consider that, although they have awarded to Messrs. G.W. Robinson & Co., and to Enoch Robinson and Wm. Hall, the highest premiums ever given by the Association, it is their privilege, in addition thereto, to record the great satisfaction, with which they examined the articles exhibited, and noticed the great improvements made by them since the last Exhibition, especially in Locks; and the Committee are unanimous in their opinion that those, of both high and low cost, are better adapted to the wants of their fellow countrymen, than those from any other manufactory in the world.

877. ENOCH ROBINSON & WM. HALL, Boston. Patent Locks; a very valuable invention. Sash Fastening; a good article. French Window Bolts; Shutter Fastenings; Spring Latches, &c. All of first rate workmanship. For the Locks and Sash Fastenings, the Committee award a *Gold Medal*.

These articles were exhibited as samples of those manufactured, for what promises to be one of the most splendid mansions in the United States, now in progress of erection by John P. Cushing, Esq., at Watertown; and the Committee are of opinion that they will prove to be equal in quality to any of the work or materials used therein. *Gold Medal.*

623. ENOCH ROBINSON, Boston. Superior Glass Knobs, in great variety of color and pattern, somewhat improved over those exhibited at previous Exhibitions, for which premiums were awarded. Patent Door Springs, answering the purpose intended, better than any other article known to the Committee. *Silver Medal*.

1853 (SEPTEMBER 27), Seventh Triennial Exhibition of the Massachusetts Charitable Mechanic Association. Boston.

438. ENOCH ROBINSON, Boston. Stand of Locks with Silvered Glass Knobs. The articles manufactured by Mr. Robinson are so well known, that but little need be said in favor of them here. The Gold and Silver Medals of the Association have been awarded him at former Exhibitions. For the best specimen of the Silvered Glass Knobs now exhibited, the Committee recommend a *Diploma*.

1881 (September 13), Fourteenth Triennial Exhibition of the Massachusetts Charitable Mechanic Association. Boston.

381. ENOCH ROBINSON, Boston, Mass. Door and Furniture Trimmings. For new designs and superior workmanship, a *Silver Medal*.

DESCRIPTION OF THE NEW DIPLOMA

Designed by Charles Howland Hammatt Billings, and Engraved on Steel by S. A. Schoff

IN the centre, upon a high dais, stands Pallas, (Minerva), holding in her right hand a wreath, and with her left resting upon a shield bearing the insignia of the State of Massachusetts; at her left hand is Justice, pointing out those worthy of the rewards of Skill and Industry; and on her right sits a Scribe recording their names.

On the left of the principal group a procession of artisans approaches, with specimens of their handicraft, as candidates for the prizes; on the right, corresponding to these, are figures representative of the Fine Arts, Music, etc.

The back ground is occupied by an Exhibition Hall, filled with various objects of manufacture, and a crowd of visitors.

In the centre, below the principal figure, is the crest of the Association.

MASSACHUSETTS CHARITABLE MECHANIC ASSOCIATION

Robinson & Hall Premiums, 1837–1892

1837 MCMA First Triennial Exhibition
Enoch Robinson, Diploma
George W. Robinson, Diploma

1839 MCMA Second Triennial Exhibition
G.W. Robinson & Co., Silver Medal
(George W., Ezra Blake, & Enoch Robinson)

1841 MCMA Third Triennial Exhibition
Enoch Robinson & William Hall, Gold Medal
G.W. Robinson & Co., Gold Medal & Diploma
Enoch Robinson, Silver Medal

1844 MCMA Fourth Triennial Exhibition
Enoch Robinson, Gold Medal
George W. & Ezra Blake Robinson, Gold Medal
Hall & Drury, Silver Medal
(William Hall & Aaron K. Drury)
G.W. Robinson & Co., Diploma

1847 MCMA Fifth Triennial Exhibition
Enoch Robinson, Silver Affirmation
William Hall, Silver Affirmation

1850 MCMA Sixth Triennial Exhibition
Wm. Hall & Co., Gold Medal & Diploma

1853 MCMA Seventh Triennial Exhibition
Enoch Robinson, Gold Affirmation,
Silver Affirmation, & Diploma

1856 MCMA Eighth Triennial Exhibition
G.W. Robinson & Co., Gold Affirmation
Wm. Hall & Co., Silver Medal
Enoch Robinson, Diploma

1860 MCMA Ninth Triennial Exhibition
George W. Robinson, Silver Medal & Gold Affirmation
Enoch Robinson, Diploma
Wm. Hall & Co., Diploma
William F. Hall, Diploma

1865 MCMA Tenth Triennial Exhibition
William Hall, Silver Medal

1869 MCMA Eleventh Triennial Exhibition
Wm. Hall & Co., Bronze Medal & Diploma
Enoch Robinson, Diploma
G.W. Robinson & Co., Diploma (2)

1874 MCMA Twelfth Triennial Exhibition
Wm. Hall & Co., Diploma

1878 MCMA Thirteenth Triennial Exhibition
Enoch Robinson, Silver Medal
Wm. Hall & Co., Silver Medal

1881 MCMA Fourteenth Triennial Exhibition
Enoch Robinson, Silver Medal

1884 MCMA Fifteenth Triennial Exhibition
Enoch Robinson, Silver Medal

1890 MCMA Seventeenth Triennial Exhibition
Enoch Robinson, Silver Affirmation
& Special Diploma

1892 MCMA Eighteenth Triennial Exhibition
Enoch Robinson, Silver Medal

WWW.ERBUTLER.COM

Photography: Rhett Butler   Typography: John Packer

The D. H. ELLISON Co.
MEMBER AMERICAN INSTITUTE OF ARCHITECTS
www.dhellison.com 216-631-0557 david@dhellison.com
3300
2002 W. 41st STREET, CLEVELAND, OHIO

PETER ZIMMERMAN
ARCHITECTS

MPF
MARK P. FINLAY ARCHITECTS, AIA
96 OLD POST ROAD, SOUTHPORT, CT | WWW.MARKFINLAY.COM | 203-254-2388

Photo by Durston Saylor

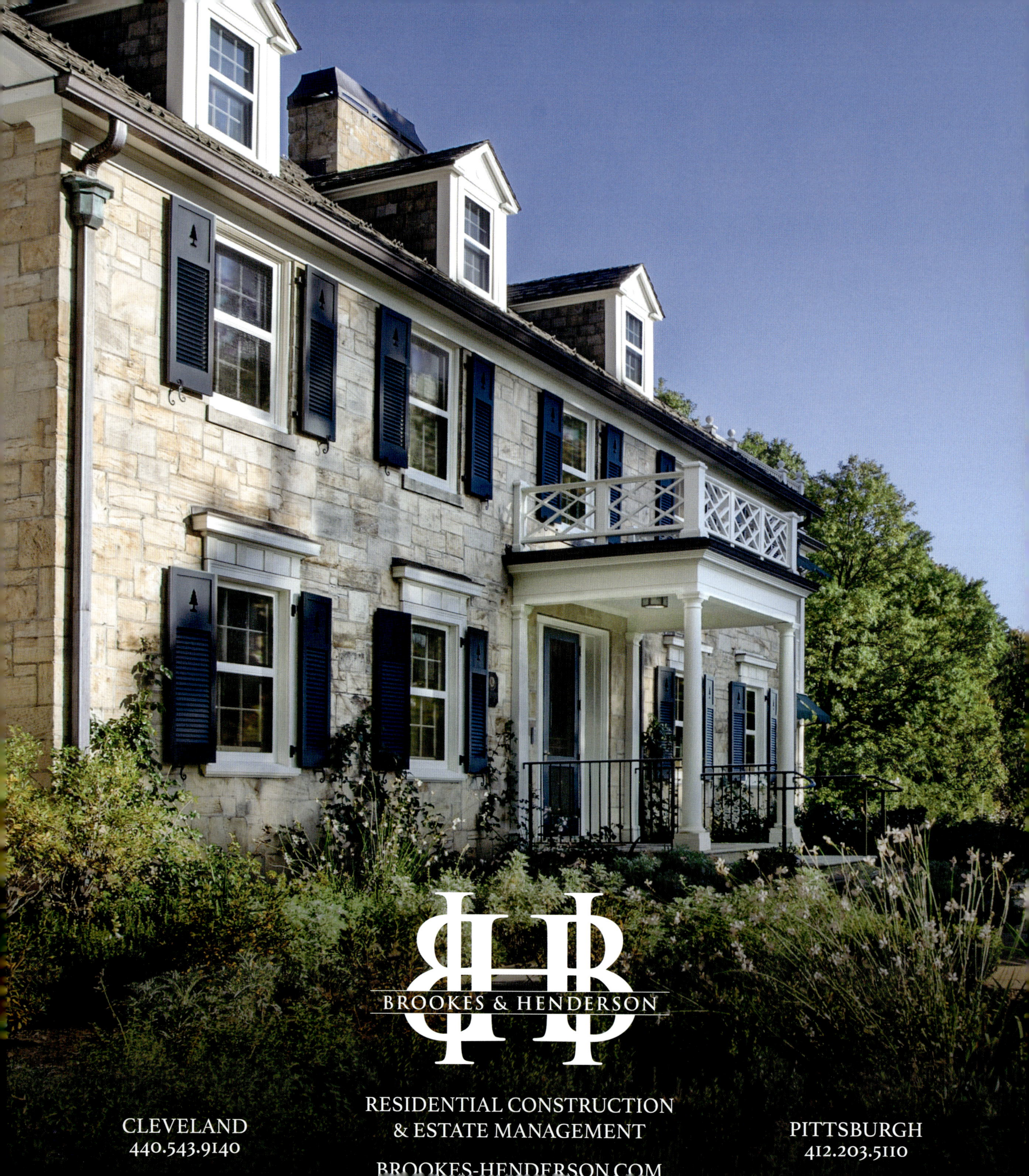
BROOKES & HENDERSON
RESIDENTIAL CONSTRUCTION
& ESTATE MANAGEMENT
CLEVELAND
440.543.9140
PITTSBURGH
412.203.5110
BROOKES-HENDERSON.COM

Photo: Andrew Frasz
FERGUSON &
SHAMAMIAN
ARCHITECTS
270 Lafayette Street, New York, NY 10012
212 941 8088
fergusonshamamian.com
@fergusonshamamian

DALGLIESH GILPIN PAXTON ARCHITECTS
EST. 1933
ARCHITECTURE + HISTORIC PRESERVATION + PLANNING + INTERIOR DESIGN
Charlottesville, Virginia
Urbanna, Virginia
Baltimore, Maryland
434 977 4480
dgparchitects.com

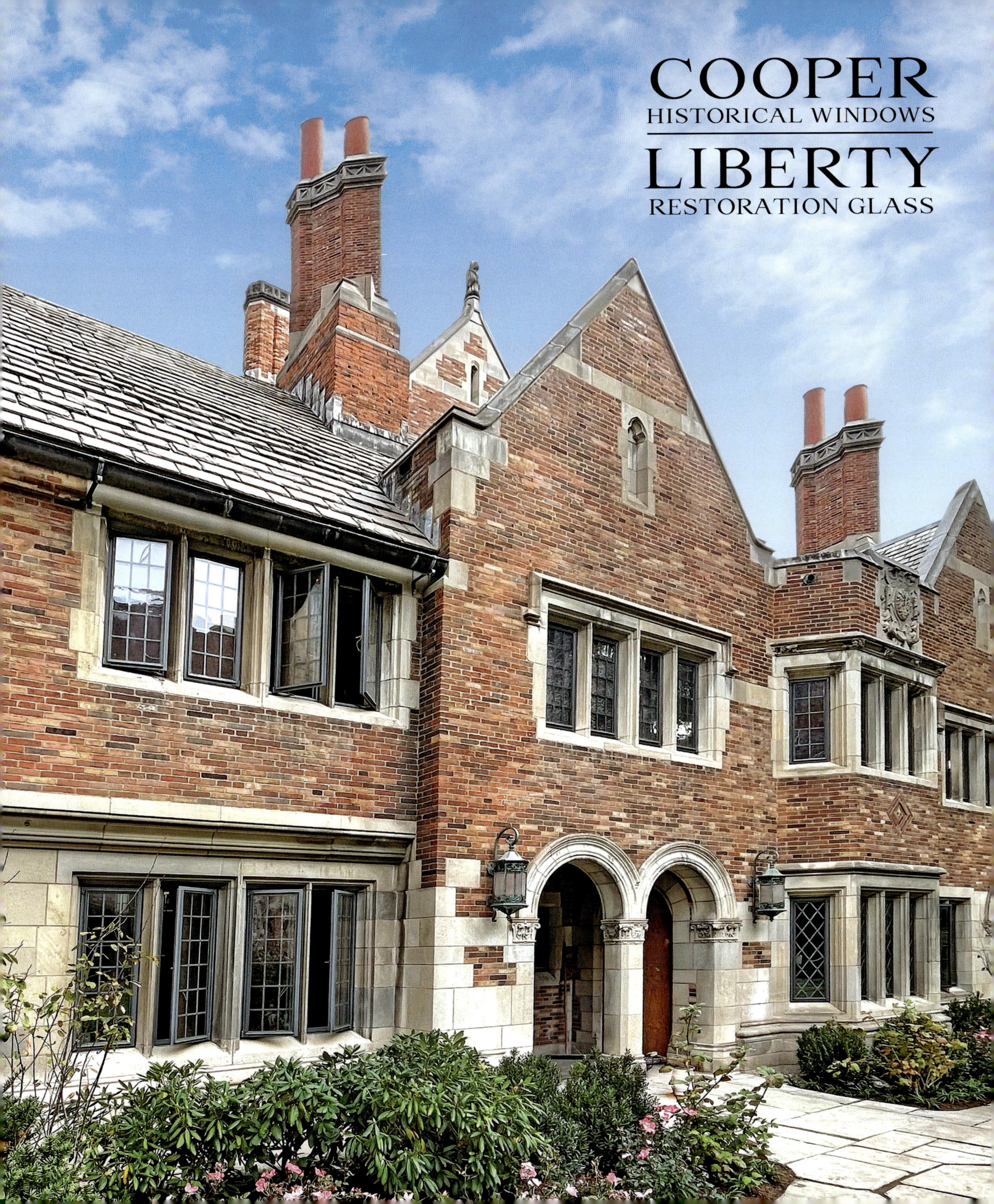
COOPER
HISTORICAL WINDOWS
LIBERTY
RESTORATION GLASS

FLOWER
CONSTRUCTION
NEW YORK — SOUTH FLORIDA
FLOWCON.NET

Debra Antolino Interiors
216.593.0060 ~ debraantolino.com

CAROLYN THAYER
INTERIORS
BOSTON
NANTUCKET
CAPE COD

JOHN B. MURRAY ARCHITECT
© ERIC PIASECKI

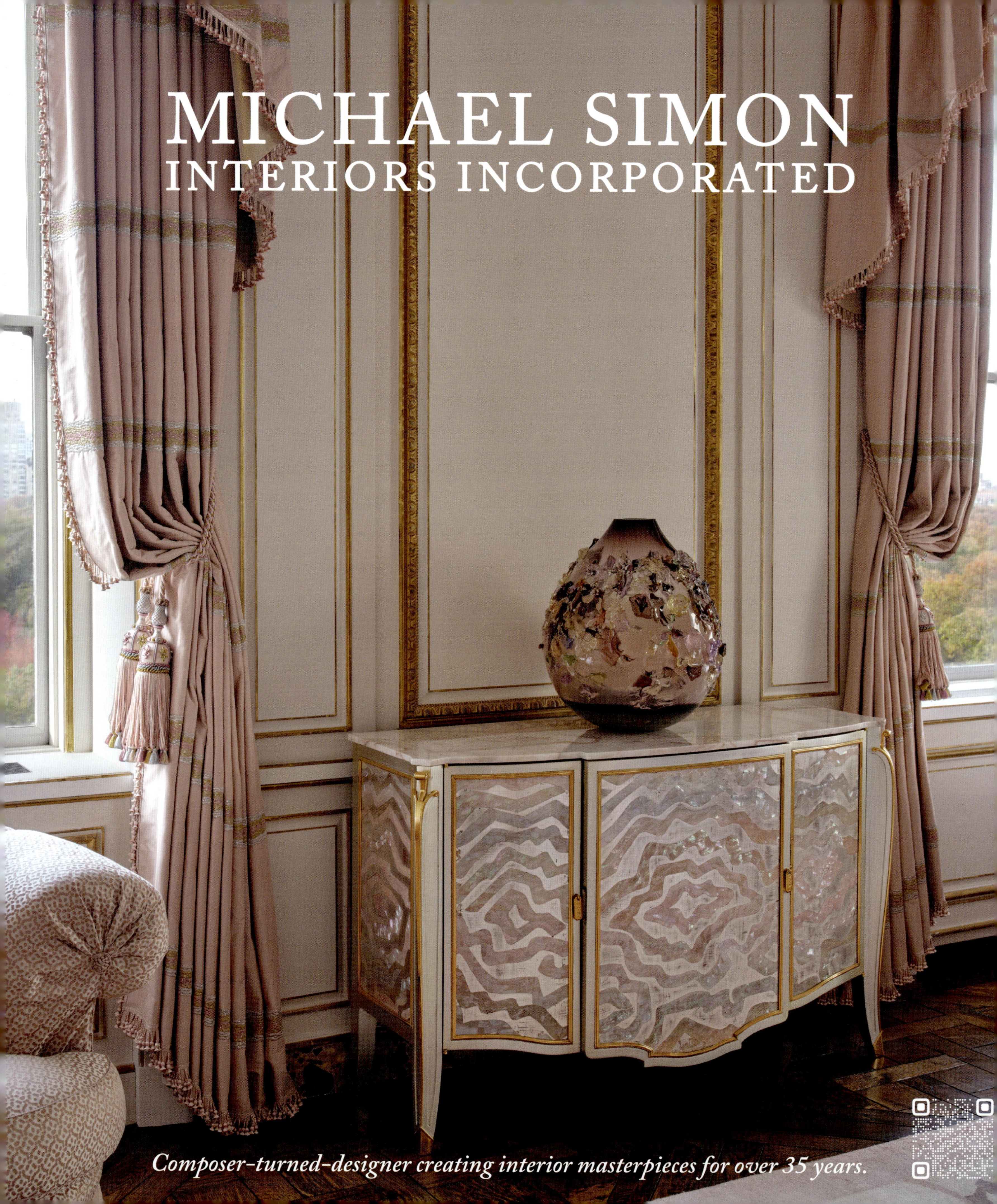
MICHAEL SIMON
INTERIORS INCORPORATED
Composer-turned-designer creating interior masterpieces for over 35 years.

DONADIC
INSPIRED TO CREATE

CHADSWORTH INCORPORATED
WWW.COLUMNS.COM
1 800 COLUMNS T +1 800 486 2118

ZEPSA INDUSTRIES
Z
ZEPSA.COM

EMILY SUMMERS
DESIGN ASSOCIATES
EMILYSUMMERS.COM | INFO@EMILYSUMMERS.COM | 214.871.9669

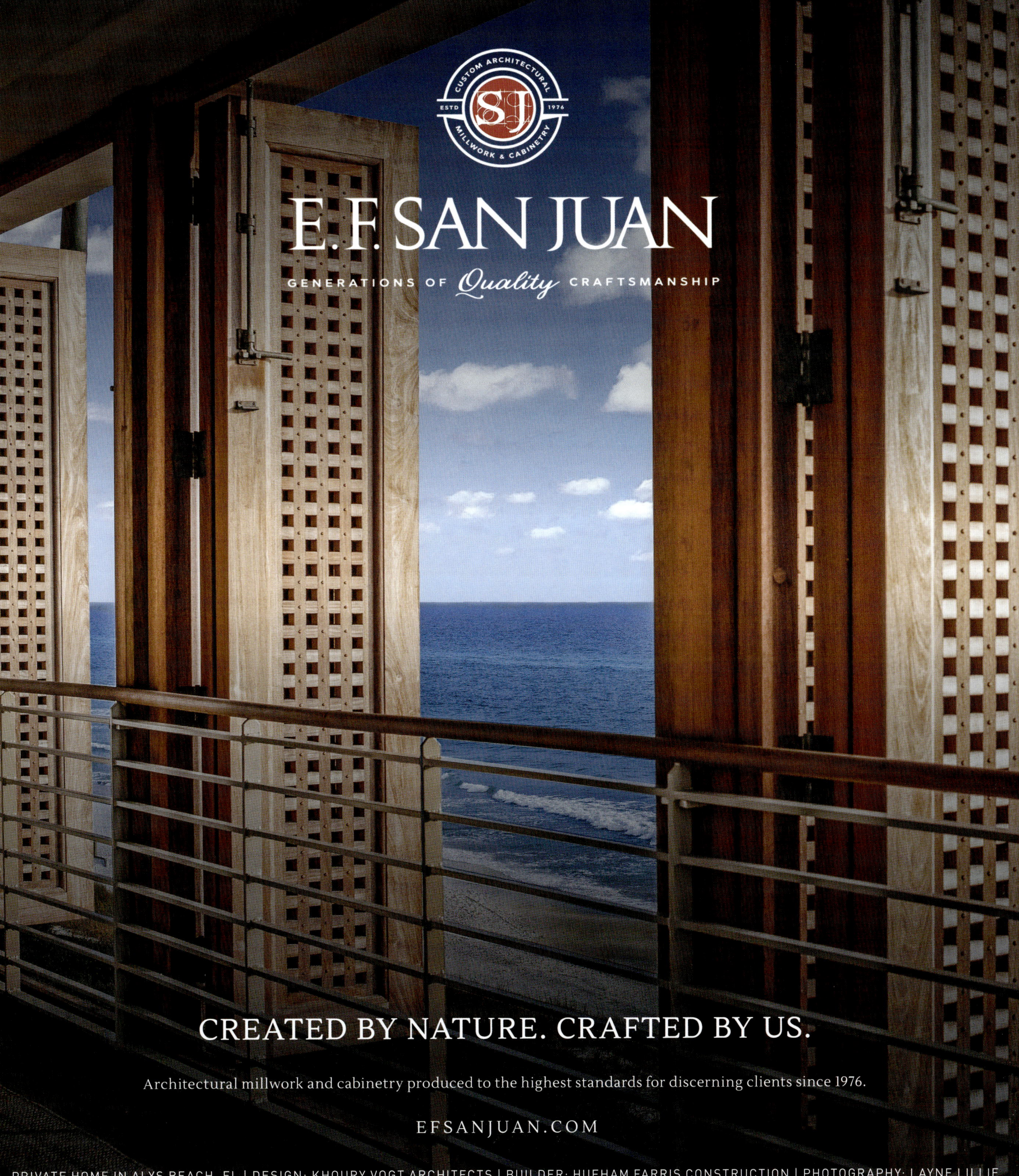
CUSTOM ARCHITECTURAL
ESTD SJ 1976
MILLWORK & CABINETRY
E.F. SAN JUAN
GENERATIONS OF Quality CRAFTSMANSHIP
CREATED BY NATURE. CRAFTED BY US.
Architectural millwork and cabinetry produced to the highest standards for discerning clients since 1976.
EFSANJUAN.COM
PRIVATE HOME IN ALYS BEACH, FL | DESIGN: KHOURY VOGT ARCHITECTS | BUILDER: HUFHAM FARRIS CONSTRUCTION | PHOTOGRAPHY: LAYNE LILLIE

WOOLEMS
50 YEARS
WOOLEMS.COM

HADDONSTONE
Trusted Cast Stone Specialists
866 733 8225 haddonstone.com

DANGORDON
LANDSCAPE ARCHITECTS
@DANGORDONLA
WELLESLEY – EDGARTOWN
DANGORDON.COM

Belt
METAL ART+DESIGN STUDIO
NEW YORK | MIAMI | PALM BEACH | NAPLES
BELT.com.co | 954 505 7400

NUDE
JOSEF FRANK

VELLA INTERIORS
BUILDERS OF EXQUISITE RESIDENCES
VELLAINTERIORS.COM ~ 718-729-0026
NEW YORK CITY

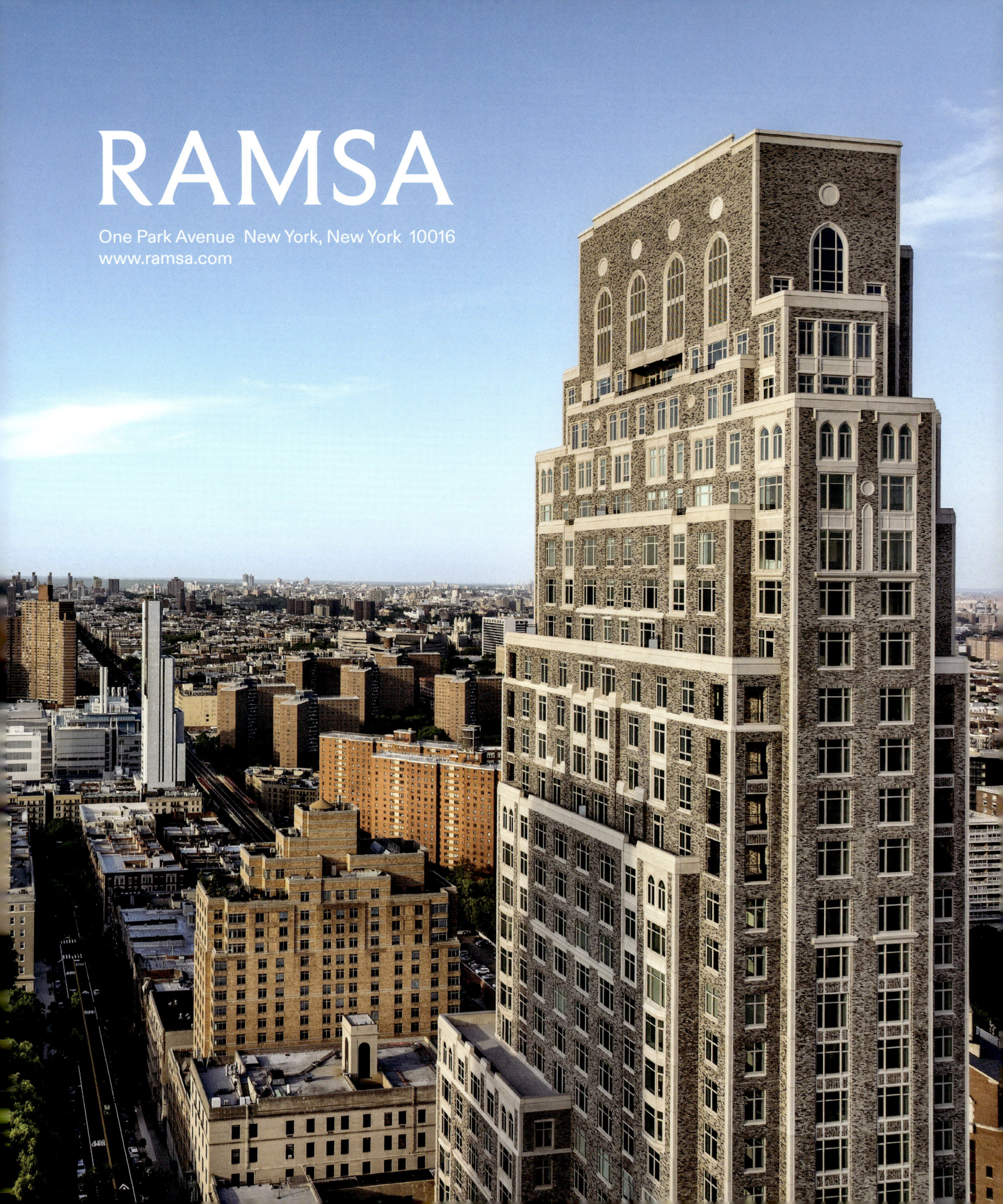
RAMSA
One Park Avenue New York, New York 10016
www.ramsa.com

To join the Institute of Classical Architecture & Art, visit www.classicist.org